THE LOST
SCIENCE
OF MAN

ERNEST BECKER

THE LOST SCIENCE OF MAN

GEORGE BRAZILLER / NEW YORK

To those Berkeley students of Sociology 290,
Spring Semester, 1966, whose sharp dialogue is
reflected in this book, and who have transcended it
by their heroic personal commitment to the issues
of human freedom and dignity in our time

The next thing to having a question solved is to have it well raised.

—John Stuart Mill

Do you think, then, that our words are any the less well spoken if we find ourselves unable to prove that it is possible for a state to be governed in accordance with our words?

—Plato (*Republic V*)

Preface

The two essays that make up this book are an attempt to explain the failure of the science of man, or better, the utter lack of a science of man in our time. They are historical essays, because the failure can only be understood historically; they are critical essays, because informed criticism is the only way out of scientific dead ends. They are an outgrowth and extension of my previous historical-critical views contained in *The Structure of Evil: An Essay on the Unification of the Science of Man;* they dot the *i*'s on my previous argument, and I think make it fairly compelling. Anyway, this is the most advanced point to which I can take my understanding of the problem, and I will have to let it rest here. It is now for others to refute this historical argument, or to do something further with it.

The essay on Albion Small is the first major critical appraisal of Small and the origins of the discipline of sociology since Harry Elmer Barnes's essay of more than forty years ago. It shows that we have made no substantive advance in solving the basic dilemmas of social science since its founding in the last century. It thus makes the beginning of American sociology a contemporary event, and it makes the development of an authentic social science an urgent present task.

The work of Albion Small and C. Wright Mills is separated in time by a half-century, but they stand side by side in accusatory judgment of the failure of social science in America. I would like to express my gratitude for unusually beneficial readings of the essay, especially to Floyd N. House, who knew Small personally and worked under him at Chicago; also to Herbert Blumer, Kenneth Bock, and Alfred McClung Lee, who were familiar with the problem of Small and its background. Their kind remarks have made it easier for me to be bold and trenchant.

The second essay was prepared for a seminar on the History and Theory of Anthropology. It repeats the basic perspective of my book, *The Structure of Evil,* and would seem redundant were it not for the fact that this perspective is kept in focus specifically on the discipline of anthropology, something I had not yet done. This is a good place to express my thanks to Gerald Berreman for his warm encouragement of these critical views, a small part of which I presented as a paper on his panel at the Southwest Anthropology Meetings in 1967. With men such as Berreman speaking out in the councils of science, we will not despair of the possibility of healing the perverse split between fact and value that has plagued us for so long.

Finally, let me address a comment about these essays to the hardheaded realist, who may smirk at their Quixotic lance splitting and utopianism. I don't see how it can be denied that the science of man is, historically and by its very nature, a utopian science. Plato saw this right at the beginning of Western history, and Rousseau revived his vision at the beginning of the modern epoch. But today we understand something these men did not: that the Platonic and Enlightenment utopianism is simply not possible—we cannot bring into being a world in which sanity can unchallengeably reign and in which self-expansive human pleasure can be assured for the masses of men. At least, this is what seems to be the lesson of our time: that the social arena is one of struggle, inequality, and irrationality, and there seems no way to overcome this, except by revolution, which in turn leads to a centralized statism that itself crushes the human spirit.

But this does not mean that a utopian stance by the science of man is unrealistic or unseemly. On the contrary, we must believe more strongly than ever in the "instrumental utopianism" which stems from 2,500 years of Western thought: that we must become as rational and critical as possible in our social arrangements and that we must continue to design, rework, and uphold an ideal vision for the masses of men. We know this will not achieve the great community of man, but it is an instrumental utopianism that alone can prevent the disaster and the death of mankind. And this is its great potential benefit.

In other words, the best we can hope for is to avoid the death and decay of mankind by using the feeble light of reason and the ideal of betterment. This reason and this ideal then becomes a way of transacting dialectically with a fundamentally irrational and evil world; they help to hold that world somewhat in balance, to "save it from itself" and its own inherent forces of destruction. The science of man is utopian, not as a starry and unreal ideal, but as what we might call a "utopian holding action" to help assure the continuation of a social pluralism of antagonistic forces.

Man's reason would then have a role that would suit its true powers in the infinity and multiplicity of the universe: it would not order that universe once and for all for the benefit of man, but would fulfill the more modest task of sustaining man in the face of overwhelming and unmanageable forces, while God and nature continue their unfathomable work. In this way the science of man and the Western dream of reason would find a natural merger with the great Judaeo-Christian and Eastern philosophies of history.

As consummate realists, let us continue to work and richly to dream, lest the militarists and other bureaucrats bend our best ideas to their age-old practical nightmares.

E.B.

Vancouver, 1970

Contents

I

THE TRAGIC
PARADOX OF
ALBION SMALL
AND AMERICAN
SOCIAL SCIENCE

*To begin with, then, teach this parable to the man who is surprised
that philosophers are not honored in our cities, and try to con-
vince him it would be far more surprising if they were honored.*
—Plato (*Republic VI*)

The name Albion Woodbury Small may ring oddly in the ears of many of us; the "period" of sociology that he "represents" may be dim in our general awareness. But as I hope to show in the following pages, there is no better way of getting at the heart of the present dilemmas of sociology than by rethinking Small's vision of sociology and by retracing the fate of that sociology in Small's personal career. If we bring him forward after almost a half-century of neglect, it is because he has something very vital to tell us about the shape of our science in the second half of the twentieth century.

In a word, Albion Small is contemporary. And the reason is that for the first time since the 1920's there is again deep searching for what sociology is, should be, or might be. The period we are now entering has all the same characteristics as the period for which Albion Small wrote. His career brings out in full relief the whole problem of the meaning of sociology and its failure to be socially relevant in spite of its unprecedented achievement as an objective science. It puts into the sharpest focus the relation of sociology to the crisis of our age. Let us explore this career and this crisis.

I The Man and His Work

The characteristic thing about Small is that he was almost universally well-liked. As a scholar, he was creative and serious; as a teacher, devoted and helpful; for tedious administrative tasks, willing and industrious; as a colleague, friendly, warm, indulgent;

as a person, ethical, spiritual. Only a certain kind of man can provoke a reminiscence like this: "It is one of the tragedies of the world that such men as Dr. Small, who so glorify humanity, grow old and die."[1] And Small was one of that rare kind; almost everyone had a good word for him. Even the historian Teggart, who reportedly had nothing good to say about any sociologist, spoke admiringly of him.*

I cite the fact of his personality because it has more than anecdotal significance: it is all of a piece with his vision of sociology. Small's whole life was oriented toward the "ethical interest," toward a desire to serve "humanity," as Edward Cary Hayes has recorded. Small was interested in scholarship primarily as a means for solving the riddle of life and trying to bring into being "the possibilities of good inherent in mankind."[2] Little wonder, considering his background: he was the son of a clergyman and had himself spent three years studying in a theological seminary.

Ordinarily we would be tempted merely to record this fact, perhaps even implying that it was an "eccentricity" of the founder of the discipline of sociology in America. We might imagine the religious and the ethical interest as part of the confused growing pains of a young science in search of itself, part of the accidents of personal biography, which have nothing fundamentally to do with the shape of a science. We *might* imagine these things, but if we did, we would be wrong; we would miss what was crucial about the very nature of sociology. The point is that Small's moral stance, his concern about the welfare of man in society, his vision of sociology as a moral science centered on man and furthering the human spirit was the original vision of sociology itself. We have only to study the articles in the first issues of the *American Journal*

---

* I want to thank Kenneth Bock for this personal anecdote and for his permission to cite it.

of Sociology to see what sociology was and what it hoped to be when it was inaugurated by Small in 1895.

We may have forgotten this climate, but it is still ours. Small's life (1854–1926) spans the era of what was commonly known in the nineteenth century as "the social problem" *(Die Soziale Frage)*. The social problem was uppermost in everyone's mind—at least in the minds of those who thought about man in society and wanted to do something to ease man's lot, or further his well-being. It was the problem of social reconstruction posed by the Industrial Revolution: the problem of building a society fit for man, fit for the optimum development of the human spirit. We may, too, have forgotten this problem, but it is still ours. Only the name has changed. Today we call it the problem of "the Great Society," but we have forgotten the stake. The stake was man, and not goods or things. And the adversary is the one whose name that we dare not breathe. Or, if we breathe it, we imagine that its ghost has already been laid. I mean, of course, the ravages of capitalism—rampant, antihuman, socially disintegrating, *laissez-faire* capitalism.

But the social problem had, so to speak, its own problem—the confused babble of voices, each with its own suggestion of a new Utopia for man. The problem was how to make sense out of this welter of "do-gooders," this morass of sentiment and confused humanitarianism. "How *do* we proceed to remedy the evils of the new industrial society? How *do* we begin to initiate reforms that will achieve concrete good, rather than merely palliate, or perhaps even worsen the human lot?" These were the anguished questions. And out of this anguish sociology was born.

Sociology was a reaction on the part of well-intentioned, scientifically minded men to the "do-gooder" confusion of the end of the nineteenth century. It was animated by a desire to base reform on sound knowledge of the social process. Objective scientific knowledge that all men of good will could agree upon was needed; knowledge arrived at through careful, patient, and serious study; knowledge that belonged to a whole community of impartial judges; knowledge that carried the force of its own recommendation, simply because it was agreed objective knowledge and not well-intentioned ideology. In other words, it was characteristic of sociology that it was born out of adversity: the adversity of the social problem and confused opinion. We might even say that these were the adversaries over which sociology had to triumph and against which it had to establish its right. These adversaries gave to sociology what adversaries usually give: a defensive posture, a negative stance, a struggle for something unusual that commands attention. But there was also another, even more formidable and even more ready to scorn and ridicule; and it was against this adversary that sociology had to react with all its might, against which it had to muster all possible respectability, all possible correctness of form, and unimpeachability of conduct. I refer to the already established and older social-science disciplines: politics, economics, history. It was these that sociology copied to get its distinctive cast as a full-fledged fellow scientific discipline, careful, objective, and, as we shall see, "disinterested."

The whole story of sociology is summed up as a tension between these two poles: the human urgency of the social problem on one end and the quiet respectability of objective science on the other. This was the "dialectic" of the development of sociology, the story of its "success," and, as we shall see, the tragedy of its "failure." Small achieved what had to be done: he founded the first department of sociology at the University of Chicago in 1892 and chaired it until 1924; he founded the first journal of sociology in 1895 (there had previously been a *Journal of Social Science* in the United States and of course others, like the Comtean journal in France) and remained its editor until he died in 1926. For objective science this was a magnificent success and perhaps the main achievement of Small's industrious and devoted career. Sociology in the United States was created as a discipline literally out of nothing, and in the face of all the adversaries that we mentioned.

2 The Early Task of Sociology in the Face of Its Adversaries

Let us examine in closer focus what Small's task actually was. The problem was how to answer the "do-gooders," by supplying a scientific methodology of the social problem. If this could be done, it had to be done by forging a scientific discipline that would complement the job of social analysis staked out by the older disciplines. If sociology could succeed in doing this, it would at the same time satisfy the critics in the older disciplines—those who, like the economist that Small somewhere mentions, would never admit a sociologist into his university. Why not? Because sociology was not "scientific," not "objective," therefore "not respectable."

But now we see the terrible bind that sociology was in: on the one hand, it had to forge a methodology of the social problem, i.e., a socially critical body of knowledge that would attack the ravages of *laissez-faire* capitalism. On the other hand, it had to do this "scientifically" and "objectively"; it had to justify itself vis-à-vis those other disciplines that were scornful of its sentimentalism and ideology.

This task was gigantic enough, but it was further complicated by an unusual historical circumstance. The ravages of *laissez-faire* capitalism were due to the fact that the pursuit of wealth had become the primary goal of American society. All social considerations—social welfare, social service, solidarity, community, social ideals—took a subsidiary position in the predominant pursuit of wealth. Capitalism, in other words, had got the social problem backwards—and this was the dominant theme of the nineteenth century. Economics, narrowly conceived as the pursuit of wealth, had won out over the problem of community, broadly conceived as the problem of human well-being in society.

Now, the further historical complication was this: the "most scientific" of the older social sciences, economics, prided itself precisely on the fact that it was a science strictly devoted to problems of the production of wealth. In other words, by following the abstraction of *laissez-faire* capitalism, the sciences of political economy in America had become "scientific"; they had an objective, quantifiable science of economics, a discipline that thrived and enjoyed the highest respectability, partly precisely because it performed so uncritically in the service of the system that produced wealth. Thus the abstraction of economic man was at the heart of both the social problem and the disciplinary problem: the concrete, living human being, who should have been the center of concern of both society and social science, had been lost in the mad scramble for wealth and in the subtle scientization of this scramble.

This meant that sociology, in order to do what it had to do both ethically and scientifically, had to oppose the older social sciences, even while trying to win favor in their eyes. Small's task was to put man back at the center of science and the center of the social problem, in place of the abstractions of both society and the older disciplines. And in order to do this he had to show how the older disciplines were failing to see the problem of the human reality in sufficient depth, breadth, and richness. He had to show that economic analysis by itself was superficial, that economic problems were interrelated with everything else in society, that society was whole, and that social relations were prior to and superordinate over economic facts. No wonder the narrow classical economist wanted no part of sociology! Sociology was out to establish itself at the expense of everything he prided himself on as a scientist (and often, as a citizen). This fact, as we shall see, was crucial in influencing the outcome of sociology's career as a discipline.*

For Small, the problem was clear. He saw the ethical bankruptcy of the profit economy, its waste, inefficiency, injustice, exploitation. He was against the inheritance of immense fortunes and the fiction of property as a divine right. He was for the production of goods for service and not for profit. The chief enemy, then, was the individualization of *laissez-faire,* the breakup of community, solidarity, and service. Small's position was very near to socialism, and Harry Elmer Barnes ranks him as just as relentless a critic of conventional capitalism as were Veblen or Tawney.† Small's problem was how to make this critical position scientifically respectable, and all his major work can be approached in this sense. It breaks down into two interrelated aspects. The first is the series of his-

---

* It is true that from at least 1885 on, many economists themselves were in opposition to the narrow idea of "economic man" and to the strict tenets of *laissez-faire* economics. As we shall see later, these were the men who founded the American Economic Association along lines suggested by the German *Sozialpolitik* tradition. The same economists had to struggle for their own scientific legitimacy and for the validity of statistical and historical method in economics. Thus the whole atmosphere of social science in these decades was one of struggle for legitimacy against adversaries, and sociology was a scientific newcomer over whom everyone wanted to lord. The A.E.A. quickly lost its early flair of social-problem "radicalism" and settled down to more limited scientific aims. The discipline of sociology found that it had to secede from the A.E.A., the very organization that was founded to broaden economic thought in a social direction.

† Small was against *laissez-faire* capitalism, but he compromised with corporate capitalism. In a recent essay Dusky Lee Smith takes Small and other leading early American sociologists to task for this compromise (see "Sociology and the Rise of Corporate Capitalism," *Science and Society,* XXIX, 1965, 401-418). This is an important and timely reminder about the failure of "liberal" sociologists generally to come to grips critically with the realities of their own social system. Yet, with regard to Small, such an indictment can be distortingly simple, as I hope this essay will show.

torical books he wrote, which attempted to put the economic problem into a broader moral perspective. It did this, on the one hand,
by showing what had happened to political economy in England
and America in the nineteenth century—how it narrowed down
from its original rooting in moral philosophy and became simply
the theory of the production of wealth. On the other hand, Small
showed how the development of economic thought in its optimal
scientific sense was inseparable from the problem of social relations
as broadly conceived by sociology. For this he used, as we will see,
the example of Germany from the sixteenth century to the
twentieth.

The second aspect of Small's work (to which we will return
later) is the longer-range problem of the science of sociology considered as a discipline. This was the problem of showing all social
things in their broadest interrelationships and, in the web of these
interrelations, placing man at the center, with his own subjective
valuations, or "interests" and "wants" as they were called. The
long-range task of sociology was to spell out as objectively and
precisely as possible what the nature of human values were and
how they influenced the functioning of society. Today we would
call this "action theory." And we may need to remind ourselves that
the problem of viewing the social system as an interrelated whole,
as well as the problem of human values seen from within the subjectivity of the social actor, are questions that have existed from
the very beginning of modern sociology, and can hardly be said
to have begun with Talcott Parsons (as has been suggested).

The First Aspect of Small's Work

It begins with his 1907 book, *Adam Smith and Modern Sociology: A Study in the Methodology of the Social Sciences*. Here,

striking out against the narrowness and abstraction of classical economics, Small frankly says that sociology is moral philosophy. In his words: "Sociology, in its largest scope, and on its methodological side, is merely a moral philosophy conscious of its task, and systematically pursuing knowledge of cause and effect within this process of moral evolution."[3] (We shall see later how crucial this definition still is.) The burden of Small's argument was to show that for Adam Smith the economic was actually a part of the moral and that the nineteenth century had gone astray to take wealth all by itself and overlook its connection with the problem of social morality—a connection that Smith had not overlooked and with which, according to Small, he was principally concerned. The lesson of Smith's life, then, is that economic theory is a "portion of moral sciences," instead of the fallacy held by Smith's followers from Ricardo on, that economics is "both the corner-stone and key-stone of moral science." Moral science is the more fundamental one, and the whole development of the nineteenth century had to be reassessed with this in mind. "Economic theory, in England and America, throughout the nineteenth century, made the wealth interest unduly prominent in the process of moral evolution, and thereby introduced confusion into the whole scale of moral valuation . . . [my argument] . . . is that a sufficient interpretation of life to be a reliable basis for social programs must express economic relations at last in terms of the whole moral process."[4]

Small actually caused a tremendous turnabout in the evaluations of Adam Smith in his time (and today as well) and made him practically a radical. "If Adam Smith had lived until today, and had reiterated certain of his general views about the fundamental conditions of economic relations, he would be classed as a socialist, without benefit of clergy." Again: "If he had lived until the [industrial] revolution was fully accomplished, he would, without much doubt, have returned to some of the fundamentals in his moral theory as a basis for restatements of the derived doctrines which have been used to bolster capitalism. . . ."[5]

Thus, concludes Small, economics without sociology is sterile science, precisely because it overlooks the moral problem. Using Adam Smith as a sort of historical paradigm (as we would say today), Small laid out the task of sociology: "Modern sociology is virtually an attempt to take up the larger program of social analysis and interpretation which was implicit in Adam Smith's moral philosophy, but which was suppressed for a century by prevailing interest in the technique of the production of wealth."[6] (Let us pause to remind ourselves about how sociology had to cast itself in an unfavorable light vis-à-vis the older disciplines, if it was to carry out Small's program. As moral philosophy it could hardly be "scientific"; as a criticism of the production of wealth as a primary social goal, it could hardly be socially respectable; as an attempt to round out and broaden the central social-scientific discipline of economics it was impudently threatening established scientific values, as well as social ones.)

Small kept up his attack and his program with a scholarly historical work two years later, in 1909: *The Cameralists: The Pioneers of German Social Polity.* Here he showed how the economic problem in Germany had been cogitated as a unified social problem since the sixteenth century, and that society and social welfare had to be conceived as a whole and not in the anarchic, individualistic terms in which *laissez-faire* economics conceived them. The Cameralists were social planners of a sort, who had a synthetic view of society; even though their planning was for the coffer of the Prince and not for the happiness of the private citizen, they did set the tone of German thinking about man in society, which was maintained right through the nineteenth century. Man had to be seen in relation to society as a kind of organic whole; economics was subsidiary to the social moral web of relations, seen in its largest scope.

The best way for Small to develop this line of criticism would be somehow to show that the facts about man, as discovered by science, stand in judgment on the narrow approach of the older social sciences. In a word, the sociological understanding of man at the highest point of its sophistication thus far shows that man is not the objectivized abstraction depicted by classical economics, but a living, concrete, valuing member of a network of social relations, conceived as an organic, moral whole. And this Small did in his 1912 article "The Present Outlook of Social Science" and in his final book *The Origins of Sociology* (1924). In between, in 1913, he turned out a blistering critique, in narrative form, of capitalism: *Between Eras from Capitalism to Democracy*. The book is difficult to read today, partly because of the style, partly because we want our scientific criticism more concise and direct. Besides, Small was not a literary man. Nevertheless, the weight of criticism is there, and Harry Elmer Barnes considered the work one of Small's most important.*

The Origins of Sociology put a natural crown on Small's lifework and in effect did everything that could be done during his time to give scientific facts social-critical weight. Small used the development of political-economic theory in nineteenth-century Germany to show that the best methodical understanding of man was itself a criticism of *laissez-faire* economic and social theory. Thus he indicated how Savigny discovered that all human things were historical creations; how Eichorn accented the interrelatedness of all social phenomena; how Roscher used a comparative method to show the relativity of social practices; how Menger and Boehm-Bawerk showed that economic phenomena are mental, subjective phenomena and not material, objective ones; how Knies showed that political economy is a moral science, just as Adam

* As did Professor Everett C. Hughes, who also told the author that Small offered a course around the book, which he called his "novel."

Smith had known earlier, but which Ricardo and his followers down to Mill had forgotten; how Wagner and Schmoller insisted on the primacy of the ethical aim of civilization; how Schaeffle had stressed that goods were means to a better life for man and not the end of life itself. Finally, he used Von Mohl and Ahrens to bring out the idea that sociology was a science of society in the largest sense.

This was the paradigm tradition continually referred to by Small in various writings all through his life; it showed everything in simplest and clearest focus and in logical, developmental historical sequence. Man was inseparable from his history and his society; society was a moral community primarily and not a wealth machine; human valuations were not fixed once and for all time— they were relative between societies, and they were subjective in each society. Man could not be approached by objective counting but had to be approached from within. The problem of social science was that of securing the good life, and for this, sociology had to cogitate man in the largest possible scope: ends and not only means; well-being and morality and not only goods. So much was this program and these discoveries part of Small's whole life that at the end he confided that if he was to be remembered in the future, he would like it to be said, "He had something to do with laying the individualistic superstition."[7]

The Second Aspect of Small's Work

When we understand the whole thrust of the major historical books that Small wrote, we understand the first aspect of his work, and we can see, too, how directly and integrally it leads into what I have called the second aspect: the longer-range, purely disciplinary pursuit of the science of sociology. And it is here that we come to grips with problems that transcend the possibilities of Small's life and his historic period. It is here, too, that we come upon that towering giant of American sociology, the only American who seems ever to have merited the title given to him by an admiring disciple—"the American Aristotle"—Lester Frank Ward. Everything vital that Small admired and found in the historical development of German political-economic thought was in some way also contained in Ward's monumental work. Ward's sociology was a reaction against Herbert Spencer on the basic points that were posed by the social problem and by the scientific development of the German *Sozialpolitik* tradition.

Spencer had understood nature and man in terms of mechanics and biology; he was embarrassed by the phenomenon of mind and admitted that he could not explain its emergence satisfactorily with his physical system. He had presented a vast evolutionary scheme in which man had a place, but in which he was dwarfed by the automatic, deep-going and unconscious functioning of natural forces. It was a Darwinian, evolutionary counterpart to the Newtonian clockwork universe, and it had the same fatal caution appended to it: trust in the invisible forces; above all, do not dare interfere with this vast and integral functioning. Nature was ordered, but at the expense of forbidding human tampering. Spencer's sociology was thus the perfect complement to the narrow classical economics, and it is little wonder that he was feted toward the close of his life at a special reception in New York. Here was the great genius who had provided the New World with a "*laissez-faire* sociology."

Ward and Small, on the other hand, declared right at the outset that American sociology should follow the French and German traditions and not the Spencerian one. And sociology could do this by sticking to the two basic points of Ward's system, which were in reaction specifically against Spencer. In the first place, Ward held that psychic forces, and not mechanics, influence human associations, that man is primarily a psychological being and not a physiological one. This meant that the task of sociology was to get at the meaning of human experience from within human valuations; it could not get at this meaning in an external, objective, abstractive, or mechanical way. Society is an arena for the play of these psychic forces in all their breadth and complexity. Sociology is thus the science that thinks of the human reality as a broad, interrelated whole; it aims to understand why men's efforts take the turn they do when men live in society, and it aims to understand this on the basis of man's subjective valuations.

Since this was true, the second emphasis of Ward's system followed naturally: sociology is the science of actual control and prediction of social events. It is a science of purposive mind, not passive matter. Sociology is a "telic" science, a science in the service of human well-being and progressive development. The central fact of sociology, as Small never tired of repeating, was "the evolution of persons." Sociology exists to get the objective facts about human association, but once it gets these facts, once it finds out what is going on in society, it must put its findings in the service of man.[8]

Small Versus Ward

Here we have, then, the two aspects of Small's work—the social problem and the scientific problem—both related, indeed, inseparable. An imposing structure for one's lifework, a fine balance between ethical and scientific preoccupations, an esthetic whole, in which a man of large sentiments and serious devotion to truth could feel eminently at ease. It represented both an attack on what Small was against—namely, the ravages of *laissez-faire* capitalism

—and a program for what he was for—a careful, objective science in the service of human well-being and the optimum development of the human spirit. It was, in a sense, a perfect middle-of-the-road attack on everything that troubled the conscience of the nineteenth century, while at the same time a perfect aspiration toward everything the nineteenth century had promised. It held the promise of social criticism without ideology—either Spencerian or Marxian. In a word, it held up the hope of ethical social criticism from within objective science. Sociology would win out precisely where the older disciplines had gone astray; instead of treating persons as almost incidental to the findings of science, Wardian sociology would place man back at the very center of scientific concern. The whole thing was so beautiful it almost seemed too good to be true. And it was.

The problem that Small posed for himself proved to be an irresolvable contradiction: he simply could not have everything he wanted, everything he hoped for. We stated earlier that Small created a discipline of sociology literally out of nothing and in the face of powerful adversaries: on the one hand, the mocking solidity of the older social sciences; on the other, the urgent and overridingly important social problem. As if these were not adversaries enough, Small gradually found himself facing another one, even more tenacious and suffocating than the others. I mean, the standard works of systemic sociology by Comte, Spencer, Schaeffle, Ward, out of which the discipline itself had to grow, if it was to achieve scientific respectability. Sociologists were desperately struggling in the last decade of the nineteenth and the first decade of the twentieth century to justify themselves vis-à-vis the older disciplines. As Small himself confessed in 1915, from 1892 on the sociologists had to feel their way painfully to scientific maturity, and the very heroes they championed were the baggage that hindered them most:

They [the heroes] were ridiculed by a hundred academic men to every one who was willing to take them seriously. For several years my lectures were elaborations of Schaeffle, with one eye constantly on Spencer and Ward. This is a deliberate confession that during those years these writers . . . got between me and the reality itself. While the emptiness of this work now almost makes my teeth chatter . . .[9]

What is at stake here? What is Small telling us? Something he repeated over and over again, something that became a theme in his own life and in the development of sociology as a discipline. And this was simply that in order to become a legitimate scientific discipline sociology had to renounce its imperialistic ambitions—the "sin" of amateurish overambition, to use Small's words. Ward's sociology was systematic, superordinate, unifying. Sociology was the crowning discipline, which would correlate the findings of all the other social sciences, show their interrelationships, and in that way make the data applicable to the social problem.

In its earlier days, sociology had to embrace Ward's conception by the very nature of its search for a place in the scientific sun. After all, the older disciplines had marked out everything for themselves. Sociology had to ask a new kind of question in order to justify itself: "What variations must be introduced into our ways of studying human experience in order to learn the most from it?"[10] Giddings and others then set out to learn the causative processes of society and the larger interrelationships of things. Thus, whereas history, economics, and politics claimed to be sciences in the strict sense, i.e., by delimiting their subject matter, sociology was forced into a negative, imperialistic stance. It had to deny their contention by showing that they missed the human reality precisely by fragmenting it. And it could do this only by claiming to be the superordinate science.

Needless to say, this was an impossible position for a would-be discipline that wanted to be accepted by the scientific community. Who would transact with such a monster? Who would welcome it at meetings? Who would be comfortable with its aims and findings, if these aims and findings were in explicit defiance of what one was doing oneself? This was the scientific "sin" that Small was later to castigate himself for. And this was the contradiction from which he had to extricate himself. It was physically and organizationally impossible to be a Wardian, and yet it was cognitively necessary to be a Wardian in order to launch a new type of social inquiry, a broadly relational inquiry with man at its center. No wonder it took so long. At the time of Ward's death in 1913 Small says that he was unconscious of no longer being a Wardian. One way of interpreting this circuitous statement is to say that he had slipped from under the giant's weight, but the relief was still not palpable. Sociology had left the grand designs of Ward and had contented itself simply with exploring the human phenomenon in a richer way.

But that last sentence itself rings falsely. It seems to leave the contradiction intact. And so it does. Let us go on to examine how the contradiction was not really resolved, but merely developed; how it changed from a mere contradiction into what I want to call the "tragic paradox" of Small's life, and of the whole development of American sociology.

3   The Tragic Paradox of Small's Career

In order to understand this we need only dwell for a moment on why Small's relation to Ward was so binding, so compelling, and yet so prone to make his "teeth chatter." The point is, very simply, that Small had to liberate himself from Wardian sociology in order to forge a scientific discipline that would take its right-ful place beside the others and not lord it over them. But in doing just this, it lost the very thing that made Ward's sociology so his-torically important and compelling: it lost the unity of social sci-ence that Ward's system had assured by placing sociology as the unifying crown of the disciplines. To get rid of Ward was to come into a paradoxical inheritance: one gained a new equality with the other social sciences, but one lost social science.

And this is the paradox of Small's career, the two poles of his writings—the tension between the social problem and the ob-jectivity of science. Let there be no doubt that Small himself was personally and at times painfully stretched between these two poles; it shows through all his work. How was the indignant ethical man to be made compatible with the detached scientist? Again and again, in article after article, interspersed with indignant books, the paradox shows forth. On the one hand, confession about how pitifully little was known about social reality: "As to the so-called social sciences . . . they had not passed far out of the homely wisdom stage of development. . . . On the whole, every social scientist . . . has actually, in ninety-five hundredths of his activities been a rationalizer at large, and in only five per cent of his ac-tivities has he concentrated upon close investigations of strictly de-fined problems, by use of an adequate method."[11] Here, decidedly, was the champion of the discipline talking, lamenting that this state of affairs had existed from Herodotus down to 1924, the date of his lament. But on the other hand, listen to this voice—the same man, but a different aspect of his life-problem: ". . . an inevitable incident of specialization in social science is a drag toward ab-straction as a finality; that is, toward dehumanizing of the spe-cialty. Sociologists have no right to assume that they will prove exceptions to this rule. Indeed, I foresee rather the certainty that in proportion as we sociologists become . . . efficient in the application of our technique, the tendency to exalt the immediate end at which our technique should arrive, viz., analysis of group phenomena as such, will show itself over-mastering us, as [happened to the older social sciences] . . . It is not at all difficult for me to imagine a stage in the growth of social science in which there will be sociologists no more concerned about anything beyond certain abstracted group phenomena, regardless of their meaning for human fortunes in general. . . ."[12] Decidedly, this is the "other" Small, the ethical man conscious of the social problem. The discipline, with its very promise of success as a scientific specialty, now held the forbidding prospect that it would follow the abstractions of the older social sciences, and lose man! But it was precisely in order to put man back into science, that sociology had established itself vis-à-vis the other disciplines.

We can see the extent of the tension in the paradox. The answer, of course, was to insist on the need for a unity of the social sciences, to insist on it again and again, even while pushing the specialized disciplinary inquiry. Thus Small wrote a major work on the need for unity in the social sciences in 1910, *The Meaning of Social Science*. It was a powerful Wardian statement of the need to center science on man. I think we have to say that there was an undercurrent of disillusionment all through Small's life about what was lost as the discipline of sociology developed. *The Meaning of Social Science* was written as an urgent reminder just at the time that sociology showed growing vigor, fifteen years after the founding of the *Journal* on a hope and a prayer that there would be enough contributors simply to keep it going.

The Price of the Paradox

In his important autobiographical appraisal of fifty years of the history of sociology in the United States, in 1915, Small tried to make a parallel between the period of 1865 to 1915 in America and of 1765 to 1815 in Germany. What was the similarity that Small hoped to bring out? It was that science progresses by decomposition and recomposition, that both epochs were notable for the development of a sagacious critical attitude toward the social reality. But, having developed an objective, technical approach, it was time, in both 1815 and 1915, to begin again to try to see larger units of the social reality, to accent again the comprehension of the total phenomena and not the study of mere parts.

Small's scientific balance was admirable. He knew that the discipline had to develop and indeed had a long way to go before it perfected its tools and objective attitudes. On the other hand, he was aware of the danger of separating the social reality into disciplines. Thus in 1919 the lament over what was now the *subsidiary* social problem is sharper: "After a generation of attention to abstract sociology, it is surely not precipitate if the sociologists begin to indicate some of the lines of action which the implications of the social process, as they have so far made it out, seem to demand."[13] This article is a long and searching one; it is evident that World War I had passionately stirred up the problem of the relation of knowledge to the affairs of society. Here, sociology had been at work since Small founded the *Journal*—a whole generation, as he puts it—and everything that had been accomplished scientifically was humanly and socially sterile. It was in the face of this that Small's interest in social reform actually increased as the years went on, as Harry Elmer Barnes observed.

To say that social action was "not precipitate" is Small's way of putting mildly a glaring disproportion between science and ethics. Indeed, sociology itself, flushed with academic and scientific success, had become not only cold to the social problem, but somewhat corrupt: ". . . in the universities, the decisive question has usually been, not what aspects of reality most urgently demand investigation, but with what sort of material one could most certainly establish oneself as a teacher. . . . Not a division of social science in the United States has fully defended itself against the lure of profits from textbooks . . . the more obvious deferring of the question, What most needs to be investigated? to the question, What sort of mental pabulum will the market digest?"[14] This was the discipline that Small himself had worked so hard to establish. It surely deserved the oft-cited epigram: "Nothing fails like success." In one of his very last published writings, a book review, Small deridingly called the social sciences a "pack of mongrels,"[15] each fighting for his scrap. It was an ignoble portrayal of a body of sciences, and although Small liked strong and flavored metaphor, it is evident from his whole life work that on the problem of unified social science he was always ardent. Perhaps at the end, as his interest in social reform grew, he could actually be bitter.

But this, as we are detailing, is the paradox of his life, and it is now clear why we have chosen to call it "tragic." There was bitterness in the spectacle of mongrel social sciences being used by those who wanted to shoot ahead full steam in their academic careers, and dreamed up abstracted research projects, when the very thing these sciences set out to promote, the development of persons, had been largely forgotten. But again, an essential ingredient of the paradox is that it was one Small himself created. And it boiled down, as we saw, to this: at the beginning of his career he understood sociology in a Wardian sense, as primarily a general synthetic science organizing all the knowledge concerning man, knowledge gathered by the special social sciences. At the end of his career, sociology became ". . . that technique which approaches knowledge of human experience as a whole through investigation of group-aspects of the phenomena."[16] And his outlook for the future was a sociology of extreme modesty: "In proportion as sociology becomes responsibly objective it will leave behind its early ambition for a hegemony over social sciences. . . . [It will be] a single technique. . . ."[17] It was not that Small had absolutely abandoned the Wardian position; if he had, there would be no paradox. It was simply that he did not see sociology alone as the science that would promote human development. This was the proper modesty for a "sister" discipline that had developed from the head of a Wardian giant.

What is the sum of these illustrations of Small's shifting thoughts and moods on the nature of his discipline? In all of it one thing shines through: Small was "fated" to be in the paradoxical position he was. For one thing, there was Ward himself—Ward the man. He didn't take criticism of his vision of sociology lightly. He even "read" Small and Giddings out of the profession in 1911, accused them of disciplinary exclusiveness against "outsiders" like himself. Ward offered the world a superordinate sociology along Comtean lines, and that was that. And in this sense, his failure and rapid eclipse were much like Comte's.

Ward's was the defiance of genius and the willingness to live alone with the passion of a vision. Small, on the contrary, had to live a life that was largely made up of administrative duties. Between these two life styles lies an insuperable gulf. As Harry Elmer Barnes noted, Small spent more time than anyone in the "somewhat thankless field of delimiting and justifying the province of sociology, and stating what he believed to be its objectives."[18] I think we have to conclude that he was fated, as we said, to be in the bind he was in. He seems to have been caught up ideologically in following out what he had to do—as editor of the *Journal,* as chairman of the leading sociology department, as propagandist for the new discipline, as public-relations man, as theoretical and practical technician.

Now we can draw this section with its long biographical discourse to a close and point out its heavy lesson. It will at the same time explain why we have dwelled on recording the story largely in Small's own words. We said at the outset that Ward was the third "adversary" of the hopeful young scientific discipline, perhaps the most formidable of all. Now we can understand that he was truly the most formidable. By straining against Ward and trying for a legitimacy that would satisfy the strict canons of a science like economics, Small had to sacrifice what he had cherished the most: the program of intelligent social reconstruction that would solve the social problem. There was no doubt about it; it was gone. There was no use calling for lines of action, as he did in 1919, after a generation of respectable abstraction. In the same *Journal* in which he made this plea Luther Bernard published an article fully defending objectivism in sociological method.

Small had created a Frankenstein's monster, a "neutral social science," and his own pleadings were now beside the point; the discipline was in new and younger hands. Not only that, he had forced himself into a position where he had to be judged inadequate. Did he abandon the Wardian position and come to insist that sociology was really a method, a technique? It was now obvious to the younger men that Small didn't really belong to that purer technical breed. In Barnes's judgment Small "lacked the training to function effectively as a true methodologist. What he meant, for the most part, when speaking of 'method' was in reality an attitude toward, or the results to be gained from, social analysis. . . . He was also relatively innocent of statistical methods, which was a grave handicap to his ambitious efforts in the field of general sociological methodology. . . ."[19]

There it was. Small no longer met the disciplinary criteria of sound method; he was not "expert" enough. We know that what Small meant by "method" was originally a place in the social-science sun, a look at the human reality in depth and richness so that the social problem could be treated with man at the center of concern. As we have already said, this is exactly what the older social sciences had failed to do. The crucial question was no longer asked, since sociology now had its public and scientific prestige. Indeed, it seemed simple-minded, but it was this: How much sophistication in statistical method did one need to call attention to the ravages of *laissez-faire* capitalism? How much did Marx have, or Owen, or Veblen?

The full tragedy of the paradox now seems overwhelming. Small had not only unwittingly dispossessed sociology of the social problem, but he found himself dispossessed of the "scientific" maturity required by the very discipline that he had forged! The moral of the whole tragedy is that by leaving behind a superordinate, value sociology on Wardian lines, the discipline left itself open to dis-interested scientific faddism, to the whims of each successive generation. Instead of leading a strongly unified social science, the discipline now found itself dependent—for its critical power—on the good graces and good judgment of the various scientists. And today we know only too painfully that we cannot count on these graces or this judgment when it comes to ethical matters.

Ward's system meant precisely the unity of science and ethics (even if Ward himself was defensive about the matter). Without some generalizing discipline to assume the burden of social criticism and unified focus on social problems there is no way of forging this unity of science and ethics. To "rely on the good will" of the scientific community is merely to admit bankruptcy, or to fall back on naïve hopes. Thus Small in 1915 said he would have no use for sociology if he did not believe it was "an essential factor in that veracious social science which must furnish the content of positive ethical theory."[20] But how could this union come about if sociology were defined as that discipline which deals with "certain objective structural and functional relationships," while ethics deals with "assigning values to the relationships"[21]? In this kind of fractured situation the most well-intentioned program is doomed to fail.

On the one hand, Small accused the discipline of ninety-five per cent ignorance and urged it to bite off smaller and smaller manageable chunks of reality for precise methodological investigation. On the other, he warned that no discipline could stand by itself without cross-disciplinary co-operation. Without some central unifying focus, such as that provided by Ward, the most that Small could do was to hope—to hope that science would progress by focusing on ever larger units of explanation. In this fashion, ultimately, the disciplines would hopefully get together on important aspects of the social problem. All that the sociologists had to do was to ". . . keep danger signs constantly displayed at points where abstraction threatens to lead away from the central human reality."[22]

Today we know better: It is not Small's hope or his warning, but rather the great Auguste Comte's caution that rings in our ears: "The subject matter of each discipline stretches literally to infinity." Today we know that the disciplines are more than ready to follow this infinite, separatist quest.

The Dénouement, *1883–1929*

In view of the beginnings of Small's career and the vision he held out, his later position seems more like a throwing up of the hands than anything else. The thrust of his whole life and of the discipline of sociology was finally given fitting voice just three years after his death. (Perhaps it was only his living presence that held the complete *dénouement* at bay.) It was at that time that

William F. Ogburn, in his presidential speech to the American Sociological Society, had this to say: "Sociology as a science is not interested in making the world a better place in which to live, in encouraging beliefs, in spreading information, in dispensing news, in setting forth impressions of life, in leading the multitudes, or in guiding the ship of state. Science is interested directly in one thing only, to wit, discovering new knowledge. . . ."

Compare this with Small's opening article that launched the *Journal* in 1895 to see the full distance that sociology had come. Yet it is a part of the paradox that Small himself had made this possible. In an uncomfortable way, Ogburn's words would be a fitting oration over Small's very achievement, a fit ending to a story that began in 1883, when Lester Ward warned that sociology had to be primarily in the service of man, else it would become a "polite amusement," or a "dead science." And this service was possible only within a unified social science such as Ward himself had proposed.

But discomfort over the appropriateness of Ogburn's words is not ours alone; it would have been Small's most of all. We said earlier that Small was judged inadequate as a methodologist by the very discipline he had forged. But this is not the whole picture; actually, Small passed this very judgment on himself, largely and gracefully. "I wish I could do a skilled workman's part of the work that the social surveyors are doing. I can't. I'm not equipped for it. I'm painfully aware of it." This was his confession, and it confirms Barnes's appraisal of him. But Barnes was so comfortable basking in the discipline's new sophisticated scientific stature that he failed to appreciate the height on which Small stood. Said Small: "I succeed in applauding them without a lingering twinge of jealousy . . . I warn them that their time will come." Styles of research change, warned Small, and each generation stands judged by new interests and new styles.[23] Today, after Charles Ellwood's, R. S. Lynd's, Pitirim Sorokin's, and C. Wright Mills's critical works on sociological method, who would dare feel at ease with a particular research technique, or sociological style?

Furthermore, and even more to the point of the main current of Small's life, is the fact that he himself evidently sensed over the years that the discipline was "getting away" from its own roots, from a necessary cumulative development out of the context of the social problem. He reported that he had "seasons of depression" over the prospect that the new generation would not build on his generation's work, but would go its own way. He even outlined schemes of research that would keep from one to three generations busy in order to "economize the resources" of sociology. What Small meant was that they would concentrate on the more central problems of human value with which sociological preoccupations began. But he mused that all this was in vain, and it was probably for the best that each generation follow its own nose, just as he had broken away from Ward.[24] And it is precisely because of this initial break that we have seen the inevitability of the outcome that Small made possible and that he would have abhorred more than anyone.

Thus the story of the discipline of sociology in America is the story of the triumph of a science over a vision. The vision had existed in the early American Social Science Association, founded after the Civil War to get on with the social problem. But the need for objective inquiry and scientific ambition in a sectarian sense had proved to be too strong; in 1886, when the seceding disciplines were about to scuttle the aim and vision of the association, John Eaton uttered his eloquent and heartfelt lament: "Let the warning cry fill the air of scientific associations, from meeting to meeting, that science is our means, not our end. . . ."[25]

It is Eaton's plea, I think, rather than Ogburn's, that is the more fitting epitaph for the spirit of Albion Small's life. It is this spirit that still haunts sociology.

4 The Historical Problem

If we left the matter here, our essay would be nothing more than an anecdotal lament. The history of American sociology contains a deeper lesson. The point is that the spirit of the union of science and ethics haunts not only the history of American sociology but the history of the last two hundred and fifty years. Let us now sketch this problem in order to bring out a final dimension of the paradox of Small's career. It is, as we shall see, the crucial point of the paradox, around which everything revolves; and for which, as we must expect by definition, Small could find no definitive solution. It is the paradox with which we are still faced today.

Whether we now choose to think it important or not, it is of vital significance that sociology began in the eighteenth century. And it developed out of one characteristic movement, namely, the full, deep, and anguished protest of the whole age against the jurisdiction of the Church over man. What the eighteenth century protested against specifically was the Church's appropriation of the problem of human unhappiness. The striking thing about the eighteenth century was perhaps not so much its "rationalism," but rather what it wanted to use reason for; it wanted to overcome the problem of pain and unhappiness, not in some future life or Heavenly City, but right here on earth. Now that man had emerged from "the Gothic Dark Ages" there no longer seemed to be anything to hinder the good secular life—nothing except, of course, the Church and its fantastic theory of human evil and the necessity of suffering on earth for future rewards in heaven. Diderot's Encyclopedia was, more than anything, a blueprint for achieving this new secular freedom from unhappiness and pain.

The only thing that had to be done—the main thing—was to take the problems of men in society away from the jurisdiction of the Church and place them under careful, empirical study. To show, in a word, exactly how human unhappiness was caused by human arrangements. For this we needed a naturalistic theory of the development and functioning of man and of human institutions in place of the theory of divine creation. When we had achieved such a theory we should have, *mirabile dictu,* a scientific theory of evil and no longer a theodicy. We could then map out "right action" and "right conduct" according to objective, empirical principles. We would have, in a word, a secular morality that all men of good will could agree on, since they could all examine the facts of the genesis of social ills and their causal interrelationship.

The quest began with Montesquieu, and was carried on by Rousseau, Helvétius, Holbach, the *idéologues,* and, in the nineteenth century, Saint-Simon, Comte, and Marx. This empiricism is precisely what Comte meant when he said that morality had to pass from the theological to the metaphysical and finally to the "positive" stage—the stage of the secular theory of good and bad. From Comte, as we know, the problem passed to Ward, and from Ward to Small. There was no doubt about it; very strongly at the beginning of his career Small was a linear figure in precisely this Enlightenment tradition. "I not only believe with Professor Ward that sociology should aim at the organization of happiness; but I contend that scientific conceptions of what the conditions of happiness would be are necessarily involved in the pursuit of this aim."[26] It was the full Enlightenment program. Small was going even further than Ward in his belief that the function of sociology was not only to find the causes of human unhappiness but also to design the good life. In other words, Small declared himself not only an heir of the intellectual movement of the eighteenth century in general but of Rousseau in particular. "Ethics must consist of empty forms until sociology can indicate the substance to which the forms apply. Every ethical judgment with an actual content has at least tacitly presupposed a sociology. Every individual or social estimate of good and bad, of right and wrong, current today assumes a sociology. No code of morals can be adopted in the future without implying a sociology as part of its premises."[27]

We need to remind ourselves how integral this ethical vision of Small's was with his understanding of the methodological task of sociology. When the medieval world view was overthrown, man was freed from the jurisdiction of the Church over the problem of human unhappiness. But this freedom was not won without a heavy price, which was that man had lost a world view. And now there was nothing to replace it. In the medieval scheme everything about man, society, and the cosmos was somehow interrelated and interdependent. Although tied together by dogma and ridden with superstition, it still was a unified world view. The new problem was not only the gaining of freedom by man but also the fashioning of a new unified vision for man. And this Small well realized when he began the above-cited major paper with a "demand for a unified view of life." The theme runs through all his early work. The task of sociology, then, was clear, both ethically and scientifically: to provide a view of man and society in their full interrelationships. In this way, a unified moral and scientific picture could be had at one and the same time.

Here we can understand in greater depth why Small was so insistent on the great achievements of the German *Sozialpolitik* tradition. They showed that man was a social-historical product, that customs were states of mind, projections of the individual subjectivity, that social life was unified and interdependent, and that the best knowledge about man was in the final analysis for the promotion of human well-being. In other words, the best scientific theory of man in society would at the same time serve as a sociological theory of evil. When we understood how the social system functions in an integral way, we would also be able to see how custom and automatic behavior produce irrationality, how they defeat successful human adaptation to historically new problems and changing times and needs. We would know how and where reason can and should be applied to replace the outworn habitual behavior that constricts the human spirit.

As we saw, the burden of Small's vision of the interrelatedness of man and society was his critique of the production of wealth, since it had submerged social service and the possibilities of truly ethical living. It was the narrow view of economic man that was responsible both for skewing the picture of man in society and for the evil that resulted from this skewing. Man could never progress toward greater good, toward a realization of the moral possibilities inherent in group life and in his very spirit unless he understood things in a new unified way. As Edward Cary Hayes insisted, until the very end of Small's career "he has regarded his own work as bearing whatever significance it possesses as part of the progress in developing this realization"[28] (i.e., of the unity of things for furthering ethics).

The Break-up of the American Social Science Association

Now we can understand what this seemingly personal scientific, humanitarian sentiment really is. It is the crown of almost two and one-half centuries of human aspiration: to replace the medieval world view with a new one in the service of man. And Small saw that sociology above all would be the science that would help secure this. Ah, yes—but let us not forget the paradox. We saw in the last section that Small, in abandoning Ward, had in effect opened the breach in his whole lifelong hope of a unity of science and ethics. But the real failure, as we also noted, antedated Small; it began with the break-up of the American Social Science Association.

This was the association that wanted to integrate the various disciplines, to keep them in some kind of unity. The purpose was not only the theoretical development of social science but also the practical problems of social reform, which had come so strongly before the American conscience as a result of the Civil War. Here was a new impetus to build a "Great Society" for the American people. The association, as Luther Bernard reminded us in his exhaustive study of the social-science climate of that time, grew out of the older American Social Science Movement. It was the failure of that movement and the utopianism it represented that gave birth to a less radical, less revolutionary or utopian approach to social reconstruction. The American Social Science Association was content to work within the present government and its political and economic structure. It wanted simply to reform outstanding abuses, working largely through education and private reform organizations. It was a "relatively conservative movement."[29]

But even this could not save it. The thrust of that whole period, from 1865 to 1915, as Small showed, was the thrust of disciplinary fragmentation and specialization. There was a need to explore the complexities of social reality. The attempt to impose a unity on the social sciences for the purposes of social reform seemed to hinder the freedom demanded by the disciplinary quest. Unity, in short, was not the spirit of the age, and the association broke up officially in 1909 after the many disciplines had already pulled away from it during the preceding decades.

Small hoped that the date 1915 would see the beginning of new attempts at unity, and Luther Bernard later thought that the period 1925 on would see new attempts at unity. In his recent 1965 presidential speech to the A.S.A. Sorokin hoped that 1965 on would see new attempts at unity. And so it goes. The decades stretch into half-centuries, which form neat periods in our imagination on which we try to impose some kind of form, and in which we try to read some kind of trend or message. But it is all in vain thus far. Ever since the break-up of the association there has been no really successful attempt to give the disciplines a significant unity. The Encyclopedia of the Social Sciences of the early 1930's was a brave try, but it lacked a synthetic unifying principle. The new Encyclopedia taking shape today, a generation later, promises to be even more devoid of any genuine internal unity. I think, in fact, that the pretense to unity is not even being made.

The Crippling of the Institut National

With this long history of failure there seems to be no purchase on the problem. We might be led to imagine that the problem itself exists only in our imagination, or that indeed there is no possible solution. How could the sciences themselves supply a unitary vision to replace the lost medieval one? How could this vision, even if fashioned, be brought to bear on social problems? Fortunately for us, there is an exact point in history to which we can trace this problem, and where we can see the initial failure. And we can see that the later failures are merely repetitive echoes of an earlier and more serious one, the most critical one of all—the famous Institut national, and its world-historical innovation: the section of "social sciences."

When this section was suppressed by Napoleon, the dream and the possibility of supplying a unified scientific vision to replace the defunct medieval one was first scuttled. And with it was scuttled also the possibility of directing scientifically the course of nation building after the French Revolution. Napoleon's seemingly peevish and impulsive act may seem to us an historical footnote on the main course of nineteenth-century history. But it is far more significant than we dare admit. It signifies that right at the beginning of the modern scientific study of man in society, social science was deprived of the two things it most needed in order to fulfill its promise. The first was the central unification of the disciplines on man and for man. This was really the instrumentation of the vision of the Encyclopedia, with which the whole French Enlightenment began. The second was the national legitimation of critical social-scientific findings by providing them with a central place in the national sun and permitting them full leeway to influence national legislation and social action. With this the thrust of the French Revolution would find its natural consummation in the crowning of the whole Age of Reason; the new nation would be directed by the National Brain.

The promise was immense and, in terms of our dilemmas today, unbelievable. It meant that the new society would be guided by a unified scientific view of man. And it would be instrumented by giving social scientists the support and encouragement to bring their findings to bear on national political questions. In other words, right at the beginning of social-science development there was held out the possibility of building a truly scientific experimental democracy in the only way it can be built, namely, by making a unified social science the main lobby on the legislative and governing process.

The *idéologues* were the new scientific liberals, and in the many key legislative posts they filled they exercised their social-scientific identity. When Napoleon began to use increasingly capricious power, the *idéologues* showed their basic antiauthoritarianism; they would not become his new political ideologists.* Thus the scorn

---

* The word *idéologues* really translates broadly as "social scientists": they were *idéologues* in opposition to metaphysicians. They wanted to build a broad, empirical picture of man as an ideational being in society.

he heaped on the "ideologists" is really a cruel twist of meanings; he was scornful of the social scientists precisely because they would not change with the political weather.* He saw the danger of social science to unreflective political power at its critical point. When he suppressed the Classe des Sciences Morales et Politiques, the social-science section of the Institut, in 1803, he really cut the heart out of its possible social-critical function. It could no longer serve as a central clearing house for the organization of knowledge, a center that would use the latest knowledge in the design of national education and for the direction of the national life. The scientific life could no longer build and support the national; by cutting away the social sciences a truly unified view of man in society and history was not possible.

The physical, natural, and technical sciences that remained were not capable of supplying a complete, new world view, just as today they are not capable of supplying it. When Guizot reinstated the social sciences into the Institut in 1832, there was an entirely new climate. The impetus of the Revolution was over, reaction had already been allowed to set in, and the new industrialism was rushing ahead under its own steam. In a way, we can understand the heroic efforts of Saint-Simon, Fourier, and Comte to provide scientific direction for the new society as an attempt to succeed where the Institut had failed. But by 1832 nearly three decades had elapsed, and there was no way to get back institutionally into the central direction of the national life. What began as a possibility of social scientists directing the national education and accepting parliamentary positions as scientific personnages, ended with Saint-Simon standing on street corners and passing out leaflets

* See Georges Gusdorf's epoch-making historical study: *Introduction aux sciences humaines: essai critique sur leurs origines et leur developpement* (Paris: Les Belles Lettres, 1960), p. 279. The basic source work on the *idéologues* is still Picavet's *Les Idéologues* (Paris: Alcan, 1891).

printed at his own expense, Fourier waiting patiently in his room for years for some interested industrialist to come and adopt his system, and Comte giving his *Cours de philosophie positive* privately to a small group of interested people. Social science had been deinstitutionalized for a fatal generation, and it found itself where it still is today: begging for attention around the fringes of national life. Guizot's readmission of the classe des Sciences morales et politiques seems to have its analogy in the English granting of universal suffrage only after the die of the new society had been safely cast.

I mention this episode in modern history because it is integral to Small's lifelong preoccupations, and his failure. As we said, the later failures to bring to bear a unified vision on the social problem are merely echoes of the failure of the Institut national. And, like it, they failed because of the victory of their opposition, and not because of any internal insufficiency. The Institut failed because it was opposed by the state. The American Social Science Association failed because the several disciplines chafed under its central direction and its practical orientation to the social problem. It was not strongly enough institutionalized as a national center, integral to the public life; it was in effect a private affair for the most part and a basically conservative one.

The failure of the association can, in a direct way, also be traced back to Jefferson's failure to establish a National Academy and National University to be located right at the heart of national administration in Washington. Jefferson was heavily influenced by the *idéologues* (he even spent his own precious time checking the galley proofs of a translation of de Tracy's treatise on economics); he wanted the best intelligence to guide the national life. But this project, too, failed, because of the pull of decentralization. Lester Ward, later, spent years trying to revive the idea of a national university, but to no avail. Need we remind ourselves that as a result no American university has been a guide in the national life? Scientific intelligence became, instead, a function of the national ideology, exactly as Napoleon had wanted and succeeded in doing in France.

The Change in Platform of the American Economic Association

This is nowhere more clear than in the fate of the American Economic Association, which we mentioned earlier. When it was founded in 1885, it dedicated itself to working with the state cutting into the private sector of the economy, planning forestation, investment, and so on. It dedicated itself firmly to fight against *laissez-faire* and its vision of economic man. But opposition against this socially radical reform platform within the A.E.A. itself was strong from the very first; the platform lasted only three years and was voted down unanimously. The words of Richard T. Ely, reporting on this early time, are eloquent: "One may also . . . see the alarm the statistical and historical method aroused [at the time the A.E.A. was founded]. . . . It seemed to some radical in theory, and the conclusion was drawn that it must be radical in practice. Hence the alarm in some quarters. Now everyone, of course, knows that it leads to essentially conservative conclusions in practice."[30]

In a word, Ely is reminding the successful—and now conservative—association that "there was nothing to be afraid of, gentlemen." The association, in fact, quickly shifted from practical to scientific work only; it even abandoned the public prize-essay contest that would arouse wide interest in the application of economics to the social problem. It became, in sum, a safely disinterested scientific organization.

And it is precisely at this problem—the polarization of society and science—that Small comes back into the picture. We can now understand in full historical sweep the great significance of what seems to be a minor chiding of Albion Small by Harry Elmer Barnes. It was at a meeting of the A.E.A., and Small was outlining one of the three prospects for the future of sociology. It was:

> ... the prospect of extending our advisory and executive share in organizing and conducting social experiment. ... Of the latter I wish I had the time and the imagination to speak adequately. If the social sciences could furnish a personnel incarnating the wisdom and the discretion which social science is presumed to confer, the world's concrete experimentation [i.e., that which is already historically taking place at random] would be put in charge of people trained for it at a rate never yet approached. From diet kitchens to premierships ... there is such a tendency as never was before for jobs to seek persons fitted for the jobs ... the demand factor seems to me much more assured than the immediate competence of social scientists to satisfy the demand.[31]

Those were strong words, even though they trailed off at the end, emphasizing the conducting of social experiment and the executive share of social scientists in this process. But Barnes, in his discussion of Small's paper, got right at the heart of its weakness, and at the same time touched directly on the historical problem that we have been considering: "I think I would stress a little more the seriousness for sociology of the lack of contact which it has actually made with public policy or private charity. ... I have not heard of the laying of the cornerstone of the National Academy of Social Science or noted any procession of legislators to sociological headquarters."[32]

There it was in a nutshell: the failure of social science dating from at least a century; the failure to lay a cornerstone of a National Academy of Social Science that would serve as a clearing house for the best ideas to be used by legislators. How could Small so gracefully fit sociology into the ongoing job market and talk about social demand? This is just what sociology has degenerated into today—an uncritical but sophisticated scientific technique in the service of the ongoing ideology, which stresses plenty of jobs, plenty of market, plenty of movement and ferment. Social science is an integral part of national life, but instead of guiding it according to a vision that would liberate the human spirit and assure the progressive development of persons, most of it is, instead, uncritically in the service of the highest cash bidder.

These are hard words, and even harsher thoughts, but say what we will, in terms of Small's own vision of an ethical science of society, they are not untrue. Is it possible that Small could have been naïve enough to suppose that somehow cumulative social-science knowledge would find its way into the governing and legislative process, even though the institutions of the society had no use for it, even though they themselves would be threatened by it and would have to reorganize according to social-science experimental findings? No, it is not possible that Small could have been so muddled on so critical a matter; if he were, he would not have lived the lifelong paradox that he did. The fact is that he saw the whole problem with utmost clarity, that Barnes's chiding did not expose a blind spot in his thinking, but really only served as a reminder of what Small knew. This can be found in the book that (in my opinion) marks the perfect balance in his thinking, the quintessence of his career, the 1910 study, *The Meaning of Social Science*.

Here Small poses a sample profile question, the kind that a mature sociology should be most interested in answering and solving: "Should a tendency toward centralization of the control of capital or toward decentralization be encouraged in the United

States today?" And he answers: "I will squarely face the matter-of-fact question which, if pressed to its last implications, punctures all the categorical criteria that philosophy has ever proposed; namely, 'desired' by whom? 'encouraged' by whom? Without a blush I return the shamelessly homespun answer, *Desired and encouraged by the consensus of our institute of social science!*"[33] (His emphasis.) In these passionate words, italicized and punctuated by an exclamation mark, Small shows that he knew the exact historical and technical problem of a mature social science. And he concludes in the full Enlightenment vision: "From this outlook there is nothing utopian whatsoever in anticipating the development of institutes of social science, composed not alone of academic men, by any means, but reinforced more and more by scientific men of action functioning as councils of elder statesmen, and focusing all the wisdom within human reach upon the conduct of men's affairs."[34] This was exactly the vision and spirit of the classe des Sciences morales et politiques of the Institut. The consensus of the institute "punctures all the categorical criteria that philosophy has ever proposed," because this consensus is based on a hitherto unheard-of new unified scientific vision of man in society.

Yet, knowing this about Small hardly solves our problem; it only makes it more puzzling. We now have to answer the most difficult question of all, the most subtle and evasive one. Small knew what had to be done historically in order to implement a mature social science. He knew further that a mature social science would have to be socially experimental. He knew, too, that a mature social science would have to be socially critical, critical of the very institutions and accepted habits that society thinks it needs in order to sustain its very life. Small knew all this, and yet he continually wavered. He made vacuous statements, naïve statements, almost pedantically scientific statements, which were always beside the point of the burning problem of how social science is to be given the technical means and made the central spot in the national life, from which alone it can function. To my knowledge, the only time Small mentioned the Institute of Social Science in his published writings is the above 1910 example.

The Problem of a National Institute in Small's Thought

It is not easy to explain this most puzzling aspect of the ambivalence and polarity of Small's thought. But, as we shall see, it is important to try. We must find a complex and deep reason for Small's failure to be consistently clear on the three problems of a mature social science, which are listed above and are worth repeating. It would have to be *social-experimental, social-critical,* and *physically unified and centralized in the national life.* The clue to this deeper reason is that Small's whole inspiration for his vision of social science came from Germany. Undoubtedly his continual and repeated references to the German experience from the very beginning to the very end of his career was influenced by his personal experiences. He had been exposed in Germany to the personal presence of some of the great figures who contributed to this tradition; he had married a German wife. But these are incidental to the actual achievements of the German tradition, which Small admired his whole life and which he desired to rework and import to America.

The focal point of his admiration was the Verein für Sozialpolitik, and it was this body that Small continually referred to as his model of what a group of academic social scientists should be. This was, in a word, the model for his Institute of Social Science, which would bring the social dimension to bear on pressing national problems, which would continually cut into the myth of economic man and economic individualism, which would reform abuses of the system, influence legislation in a direction of social equalization of wealth, crystalize public opinion in the direction of reform proposed by the scholarly experts. The ultimate purpose was to make public opinion effective in molding the civic and economic policies of Germany, using the ideas of academic scientists. This was the program of the Verein, and Small was lavish in his eulogy of it, precisely because it set out to lay the ghost of individualism and *laissez-faire*. He called it "the most exemplary constructive enterprise that has ever been carried on by scholars in the social sciences ... the most clearly defined, the most energetic, and the most comprehensive attempt ever successfully undertaken by academic men in the way of social construction."[35]

We said that this was the model for the Institute of Social Science that Small so strongly proposed a few pages before in the same book; at least, it would appear that way. It seems that Small had marshaled his whole vision and argument for social science on a clear central focus, and that at last we had a lesson from history, a program for implementing social science in social reform, and the proposal for a center from which all this would be fed into the national life. Alas, we are wrong; it only appears this way. The fact is that no sooner had Small detailed his argument than he slipped into his expected and inevitable paradoxical pose. Listen now to the "other" Small, and see how the clear vision is trifled away:

Whatever may have been the service of these German scholars in the way of actual social construction—and the balance sheet of this account has not yet been drawn up [1910]—their other kind of service is likely to be, for a long time to come if not always, the more instructive precedent for American academic men. By teaching, by addressing many different types of audience, by systematic publication, the members of the organization changed the valuations of Germans both about social means and about social ends. Whatever we in America may think of these valuations in themselves, they have actually been wrought into the fabric of German life. In general a parallel relation to the entire social task must be assumed as the primary calling of American academic men. Whatever we may be able to do more . . . our first and largest function as academic men must always be to help our fellow-men find out what is true, and honorable, and just, and pure, and lovable, and reputable. We shall at least have done a necessary part if we do no more than keep attention fixed on these things, while other men are doing the subsequent work of more directly making these valuations bear the ripened fruits of action.[36]

In a word, a rhetoric of hope and consolation for ineffectuality has replaced the clear vision of a National Institute of Social Science. It should now be the task of the "other" Small to console us for this muddling of our program, and this he does:

Although social science is abortive unless social evaluation passes into corresponding social action, the work of individuals which stops in one of the preparatory phases of social science need not be abortive. Division of labor may provide for its continuation by other men. No infallible means are known for transforming social valuations into corresponding social constructions.[37]

Where would we look for these "other men" who will carry on the "corresponding social action"? Why are we suddenly bereft of dependable means to transform these valuations into action? What happened to the institute? We cannot try to answer these questions; at least, we cannot try to carry on a dialogue with Small about them. And the reason, as we know so well by now, is that there are two Smalls, both talking very nearly at once, and then slowly shifting, and suddenly irrevocably split into two poles. Thus the "other" Small confides in us, after making the above qualifications in his vision, that if students had asked him twenty-nine years before whether it was the duty of professors to reform the world, he would have answered yes. But now his thinking has changed, and he offers us a different program. No, not only different, but actually a program that has failed. And instead of frankly admitting this failure, Small beclouds it by infusing it with hope.

The Change in the Verein

I do not mean that hope is beclouding, but merely that in this case it is a hope that is not warranted by the data of history. The Verein, as we noted, was the organization that inspired the American Economic Association, and the A.E.A., as we also noted, "failed" in the sense that it quickly departed from its radical founding platform. It became a disciplinary, scientific, and thus relatively conservative organization, quite beside the point of the social problem to which it had addressed itself at the beginning. If this was the fate of the A.E.A., was any better fate to be expected for the Verein? The fact is that the Verein, too, shifted from its earlier hopes. The public-opinion work that Small so eulogized as the proper function of the social scientist was something that the Verein itself abandoned in 1881. It then became simply a learned society, another private organization devoted primarily to the compiling of historical and descriptive monographs.[38] Like the A.E.A., the Verein had adversaries, and many of them: adversaries among the more orthodox theoreticians of the traditional school and adversaries among the "practical men" who possessed wealth and manipulated power. They called it "Socialism of the Chair," and they swept by its doctrine into the continuing "passions of the economic life," as Gustav Cohn lamented.[39] In other words, the more radical program of the Verein was caught up in the blatant play of economic life even while Small was praising it as a desirable ideal. When its historical method triumphed, it found that its program had been adulterated as the very condition of this triumph.*

Small continued to praise the Verein to the very last of his writings. In 1924 he cited (as Brentano had done earlier) the great number of volumes that it had already published; this was the only cumulative and last possible realistic measure of its success. Small's belief evidently was the same that had animated the founders of the A.E.A., which was that knowledge, as truth, would out. But this is going beyond the bounds even of paradox; it overlaps into naïveté. Small should have known better, at least as a lesson from World War I. The German academicians always praised their fatherland, and the war proved that they meant it. The profound shock and disgust that Small experienced over their attitude on the war only proves that the Verein failed. Germany went into World War I, and the Hitler epoch, and World War II, and today a German army of 500,000 stands posed with nuclear-armed rockets.

Does it seem unfair to draw these facts into the picture, to judge a scientific enterprise by these standards? Does the history of cataclysm negate the cumulative tradition of outstanding monographs and scientific findings? Does it overshadow so completely the fact that here was an organization that did make its weight felt, via the German bureaucracy, in the national life? Who is

---

* Lujo Brentano, writing on the Verein in 1901, quoted (oddly enough) by Small (*American Journal of Sociology*, 1912-13, p. 464).

to judge? It depends on the criterion for success that one uses. And how does one judge the success or failure of an enterprise like social science? What conceivable standard are we to use?

Why not use Small's own standard, the standard of his early days, and the one to which he returned periodically, although never so strongly as in his early Wardian vision. I mean, of course, the standard of the Enlightenment itself: that social science exists in the world to form a new unified scientific vision of man, to help instrument this vision in the governing process, and thereby gradually abolish ignorance, superstition, poverty, and war. It was this program that would fulfill the highest function knowledge could fulfill. Indeed, it would perform the main task and ambition of man on earth: the progressive liberation and realization of the depths of the human spirit. And why, then, did Small himself not adhere to his own standard? Why did he vacillate between the Institute of Social Science and an alternate program that had already historically failed? Why did he abandon the position that professors themselves should be social reformers? The answer to these questions would also provide the answer to the whole vexing puzzle of Small's career, and to the long historical problem we have been examining. Let us then focus a bit more closely on this problem.

The Historical Problem Clarified

There would have been no justification for dwelling on the several aspects of Small's career if there was an easy solution to the paradox. If we judge Small only in the light of the bind he was in, he looks ineffectual, rhetorical, and sometimes even a shade less than candid. How did a thinker of his depth of sentiment and broadness of view find himself so unable to proceed to a direct resolution of the problem of social science? And why, when once he did clearly glimpse the straightforward solution, did he not remain faithfully with it for more than a few paragraphs in his 1910 book?

The only kind of answer that would be fair to Small would be to show that his equivocation and dilation were honestly unavoidable, that he was forced into his many paradoxical poses by the complexity of a problem that would have baffled and humbled even the greatest mind. The answer that vindicates Small must be that at the end of our labors, at the bottom of the problem, we found a hurdle of such magnitude that even our best minds and most sincere efforts were balked by it, a puzzle of such a nature that social science itself would be fragmented into a dozen pieces by it. We would owe Small nothing less than this; if it were not so, it would not have been worth the trouble to write critically about him, or to cite his writings today.

The clue to the size of the puzzle, as we hinted, is his lifelong preference for the German *Sozialpolitik* tradition. We said it was "the deeper reason" for Small's failure to be clear about the form of a mature social science. As we noted, he often reminds us that he chose to accentuate the German tradition not because others did not have the same ideas but simply because it best illustrates the progressive development of this knowledge. Yet Small chose the German tradition for another important reason, and that was his evident discomfort with the French, a bias he once admitted to Ward, and that seems to have grown as he abandoned his early Wardian vision of sociology. In his early references to Comte, for example, he gave Comte prominent place as the direct precursor of modern sociology,[40] whereas at the end of his life he had this to say: "[I] . . . feel bound to emphasize the conviction that Ward improvised an entirely mistaken interpretation of cause and effect when he led Americans to believe that they owe sociology to

Comte. . . . [I contend that sociology has] little use for Comtean elements, and that the efficient cross-fertilization came from the German tradition."[41] There is no doubt here about Small's emphatic position. He was not scientifically comfortable with Comte nor, for that matter, with the whole French tradition. He admits that sociology was largely fathered by "sympathetic" rather than "scientific" people: the "sentimental philanthropic impulses" of "the Rousseau-Diderot succession," or "of the type of Saint-Simon . . . and Fourier. . . ."[42] And in his 1894 book he even devotes space to Babeuf.

But for Small, sociology was a different thing than these crude and fumbling beginnings. He never mentioned Babeuf again. When he mentions Montesquieu, it is only to compare him as a sociologist favorably to Plato, and to lump him with Bossuet, Buckle, Herder, Hegel, Lotze, and Marx. In a word, it is not sociology, but the philosophy of history.[43] Finally, what are we to make of the following words from an article in the *Journal* on the centenary of Comte's 1822 appeal for a science of society? The article is unsigned, but it is surely by Small, and it contains a very telling revelation: "So far as it is visible today, the precise truth is, first, that Comte anticipated by more than a half-century an effective demand for a sociology; second, that when the demand came it was actuated by impulses among which the Comtean tradition was not the most powerful."[44]

There is something wrong with this praise of Comte and with this easy assessment of his "precise" place in the development of sociology. It is the same thing that was wrong in Small's generous inclusion of the "sentimental" and "sympathetic" types—Diderot, Rousseau, Saint-Simon, Fourier—as fathers of sociology. What is wrong is that the standard of appraisal which Small adopts skews the spirit of that whole early period as well as overlooks the problem that the period left us. The fact is that Montesquieu fits more comfortably into the history of sociology than he does in the philosophy of history; his was the first modern attempt to detail objectively some of the factors that determine the institutions of a society. As for the "effective demand" for sociology, this was the whole spirit of the eighteenth century, voiced in no uncertain terms in the closing paragraphs of Helvétius' great work *On Man*. And what about Condorcet and the *idéologues;* here surely was the effective demand for a science of man in society at the very apex of its intensity? And what about Rousseau, with whom the earlier Small had so much in common, in his vision that the function of science is not only to study empirical facts but also to help design ideals? And what about the Abbé de Saint-Pierre, who first proposed the creation of an Academy of Moral Science in France— the model of the Institute of Social Science that Small spoke so strongly for?

When Small overlooks all this, he must have a perfectly good reason. Why does he apply such a rigid scientific canon to Comte and his predecessors? The answer must be that these people were incompatible with the kind of sociology that he was working so hard to forge—by which I mean the *discipline* of sociology. This is what he meant by the first "effective demand": the American demand for a scientific, objective, value-free, neutral discipline of sociology. And this, it is true, was something brand new, something the Enlightenment did not understand precisely because they did not want to understand it; they wanted a new unified view of man in society. It was something that Comte himself was strongly against in his insistence on the unity of science for social reconstruction through education.

The reasons that Small gives for disliking Comte are that Comte was pre-Darwinian, that his "religion of humanity" was static and unreal, that positivism was repellent in its Robespierre-like atheistic cast. These reasons are debatable, and in any case they are beside the point. They are facts about Comte that overlook Comte's position in an antecedent movement. The tradition that Small plays down is the very one that gave birth to the Institut and that staffed it with scientists trying to meet the new "effective demand." But, as we noted, by the time Comte came upon the scene Napoleon had already emasculated the Institut as an effective critical voice in national affairs. In 1822 Comte had to try, with Saint-Simon and Fourier, for a reorganization of society—a reorganization that no longer was able to proceed in an integral scientific, parliamentary fashion, using the very energies of the Revolution itself in a gradualist, progressive direction. Comte could not even get the academic post he so coveted and undoubtedly merited. Thus we can understand him in one very real sense as an outsider to a development of social science that had already been sorely crippled by state intervention. It was not just that sociology was yet unborn when Comte came upon the scene; it was that sociology in the Enlightenment vision and implementation was practically dead.

From this point of view, we can see that Comte's system was almost forced to reflect an "excess of the outsider" in a tradition that was sorely crippled and fighting for its life—the tradition of scientific social reconstruction. This is the kind of excessiveness we have come to expect from ideas that have to go begging for attention, that have to make their way in the face of impossible odds and numberless adversaries. The vision of the unity of science and life—the vision of a thoroughgoing social reconstruction in the face of deep-rooted habits—had already something of the "quack" about it when Comte wrote. The energies of the Revolution had been redirected into the most accommodating social forms.

In our day we saw Nehru miss a similar opportunity when he failed to marshal the intellectuals around the dynamic social idealism present at the time of Independence. A few decades later it is too late; idealism tends to assume more and more the pose of radicalism and the form of a finished system. It simply has no opportunity to be progressively scientific, because it is fighting for a place that the vested social interests no longer hold open to it. It is thus easily elaborated, as we said, into a finished type of world vision that is very antagonistic to the true scientific spirit, which is always cumulative, gradualist, tentative, open. And even where this world vision partly maintains the scientific spirit, as in Fourier's willingness to have his deductions proved wrong, society is no longer willing to try the experiment. To experiment socially has become "utopian."

After this "totalistic" epoch the German historical school looks like open heaven itself, and this is what Small felt. It is the same sentiment that Schumpeter expressed when he, too, said that Comte was not the authentic precursor of modern research, and asked: What "has Comte's intellectual world in common with the historical school, unless the latter is deprived of all its characteristic features?"[45] But what we want to remind ourselves of here is that this gradualist and tolerant new social-scientific attitude is itself built upon two failures that took place in France: the failure of Utopian socialism and the earlier failure of the Institut, which in a sense can be said to have given birth to the need for Utopian schemes. If science had been allowed to have a central place in the new society after the French Revolution, perhaps there would have been no need for Utopian visions. This is, of course, a big "if"—and probably an impossible one. The social forces unleashed by the Revolution swept over France and inundated all of Europe. How could a mere scientific hope take control?* The program of

* And a weak scientific hope at that, in one crucial way. There was no real synthetic unity in the Institut. Auguste Comte, for example, was glad that Napoleon had suppressed the section of moral and political science; it would only have dissipated itself due to the uncoordinated fragmentation of research (*Cours de philosophie positive*. [Baillière, 1864, 2nd ed., Vol. 6], p. 404). And as Comte lamented, when Guizot later reinstituted the section, he kept the earlier fragmentation.

the French social scientists succumbed directly to Napoleon and the state; but these were really expressions of a whole social and historical context that made it very unlikely that social science could be given any kind of vital chance.

In Germany the new tradition of historical scholarship already had a failure behind it, similar to the French failure. When Bismarck unified the nation in 1871, it may have seemed that the future of social science was opening up for the first time, that here was a new hope of working for human betterment and peace. Actually, as Alfred Weber pointed out, with the advent of Bismarck politics and power slipped away from any kind of intellectual control. Whereas German intellectuals had formerly been represented in Parliament, they were now succeeded by the new vested aristocratic and industrial interests. And so the "split between mind and politics"—to use Weber's chillingly apt phrase—really began.[46] The Verein was founded, then, at a time when active intellectual control of the public life was already a dead hope. And World War I, as we saw, was to prove how regrettable had been the failure of the *idéologues* to establish the primacy of mind over politics. It was obvious that Small's colleagues in Germany were for the most part ideologists *first* and social scientists *second*. The spirit of the earlier French social scientists—their internationalism, their willingness to retain their own scientific-critical identities in opposition to Napoleon's growing capriciousness with power—was already but a memory in the life of social science.

This is the real lesson of the difference between the French and German social-scientific traditions. Ever since the failure of the Institut and the Utopian socialists, social science has been either unwilling or unable to assume its own authentic identity, to reach back to the eighteenth century and find its own characteristic spirit, to search its own soul to find the courage of its first beginnings. In a word, social science has been unable to face frankly the fact that *its authentic posture is the posture of social criticism, informed scientific criticism of the very society in which the social scientists themselves live and work*. This, and this alone, is the meaning of the origins of social science in the Enlightenment. It was then that man most clearly saw that his enemy was anything and everything that exercised constraint and tyranny over the human spirit—either outright tyranny, as in oppressive government, or subtle and difficult-to-ascertain tyranny, as in the causes of evil in the structure of society, when social arrangements work against man. This was the program of Enlightenment science in its rebellion against the Church; it wanted to make man its own domain and the liberation of man its goal. Social science sought to find out how the social system itself causes evil. Once it found this it could proceed to its own projection of new social goals and values. Furthermore, it was helped in this posture of self-criticism by a spirit of internationalism that pervaded the age.

By the end of the nineteenth century, however, the spirit was dead, and nationalism was the completed new focus of allegiance that made it difficult, if not impossible, to turn one's full critical gaze on one's own social world. It was a long way from a nascent science that published its critical works under pseudonyms because of fear of arrest by the authorities to a discipline that at one time was known as "American sociology."

The Center of the Paradox of Social Science

And so we have come to the *dénouement* of the riddle of Small's life by following the clues of his preference for the German tradition and his denigration of the French. At the very center of the paradox was the overwhelming contradiction that the French tradition was the only one in which a truly humanitarian social science could be effective while at the same time that tradition was socially and scientifically impossible. How can social science function in opposition to some of the very basic institutions of its own society? Social scientists would have to be revolutionaries or quasi-revolutionaries functioning in a highly critical role within the legislative process. And that is the supreme paradox. How will the vested interests of society allow a revolutionary social science? How will it allow even a pseudorevolutionary one, one that would attempt to change the laws to the detriment of the vested interests? The only possible glimpse of hope for a beginning on this problem is when history itself offers a fleeting moment of opportunity, as it did at the time of the French Revolution and the Institut. But there is no way of knowing whether that time was propitious. It may very well be that the opportunity slipped by quickly because the idea was really historically impossible. It may be the ultimate Utopianism of all, infinitely refined since Plato, but still a fantasy.

This is the puzzle of overwhelming magnitude that we find at the heart of Small's career, and it vindicates Small completely of any intellectual confusion or moral evasiveness. It is the phenomenon that I have elsewhere termed "the eternal paradox of Enlightenment science."[47] If we judge social science against the vision that Small held out for it in the beginning of his career, we must see that by this standard social science has failed, and *it must always fail.* At least, that it is the way it still looks in our historical period. And this is what Small must have meant when he said that "no infallible means are known for transforming social valuations into social constructions."*

* See also Lewis Coser's recent sensitive historical probing of many sides of this problem: *Men of Ideas, a Sociologist's View* (New York: Free Press, 1965). Coser wrestles—as he must—with the paradox that the intellectual must be critical of the established institutions and ideas while at the same time

Looked at in this way, we can understand many things about Small: his odd reading of the history of sociology, some of the high points of which we have sketched, although we have omitted others, like his belief that before 1800 nothing happened in the science of society except "freaks of prematurity."[48] It was only from 1800 on, claimed Small, that a truly objective tradition was forged. We can understand that he wanted and had to have an objective tradition, otherwise sociology would show its wholly radical underside, which would be unseemly for a discipline that had to be built under the conditions that American sociology faced. We can also understand why Small, when compared with Ward and his staunch integrity in the face of adverse opinion, appeared uncomfortably accommodating to diverse pressures. Small accommodated because he had to.

So we are left with the paradox today. Social science has inherited the task of forging a unified vision of society in order to further the progressive development of the human spirit in its earthly career. But this unified vision must be in some fundamental ways critical of the very institutions of one's own society. It must imagine, plan, construct, implement, and experiment with alternative ways of living in society. In this way, and in this way alone, can a mature social science be built.

This program should not stir up the ominous bogey of a science that would manipulate people. Social science would concentrate

---

fitting creatively into the society. Needless to say, Coser cannot push the problem to any clear solution and is obliged to leave the intellectual suspended in a limbo between "total withdrawal and total integration" (p. 360). But this hardly answers his major hope, namely, that the intellectual will "still have vital roles to play" so long as the society remains "open and pluralistic" (p. 360). What exactly *are* these roles, and how will he play them from his paradoxically suspended position, even if the open society were to continue to eternity? (See our discussion of the alternatives to a science of man at the close of this section.)

on criticizing the institutional structure of domination on the range of human choice and thus would seek to alter the laws and customs governing social living, with a view to offering people new alternative choices in their lives. The center of decision would lie with the individual citizens, making it possible for man to partly make his own history and partly permit his own freedom. In this way man comes into his earthly inheritance in full measure as he is actively involved with his guiding intelligence in helping to shape his own destiny.

We can sum up our discussion best, I think, by saying that there are only four alternatives to a science of man in society:

1   The first is a *National Institute of Unified Social Science* that would seek the causes of evil in social life and guide in the formulation of national policy. This is the alternative that, as we have seen, has successively failed in history, from the Institut through the American Social Science Association, the Verein für Sozialpolitik, the American Economic Association, and various other organizations of social science. After the Institut these others have been only pale shadows of what was needed. (But let us again remember that the Institut, too, lacked the essential genuine unity.)

2   The second alternative was suggested long ago by the British sociologist Victor Branford, namely, that of a *new political party of social scientists.* This would come about as the social scientists acquired a collective consciousness of themselves as a social group with a definite and specific heritage which would be conceived as a trust. This heritage and trust would then become the idea around which a new political party of social scientists could be formed. It would seek to advocate "such policy as the sociological doctrine may sanction."[49] Given the social-critical nature of social-science findings, this party would have to be an active opposition party, combining the social-critical role of the intellectual outsider with inside participation in the democratic process. Whereas

the Institut began with the hope of immediately making science the main lobby on the legislative process, the party of social scientists would begin with the hope of gradually becoming an important opposition party as it won support from other segments of the population.

3 The third alternative is the one we have lived through as a consequence of the failure of the first two. It is the alternative of a metaphysic of hope that we cal' euphemistically, the scientific "disciplines." This metaphysic imp. es that by pursuing the disciplinary quest, we would one day somehow have a unified science in the service of man. Comte had already shown the fallacy of this metaphysic, but for certain reasons (valid and invalid) we have chosen to ignore this.

4 The price of our unruffled scientific calm is that we must forego the active experimentation in society that would firmly establish the interrelationships of things. As a result, we periodically lapse into the fourth alternative, *the philosophy of history*. This is a substitute attempt to find the meaning of life—the causal factors of history—in the natural and historical process. We need not intervene, we can content ourselves with studying and imagining. Small was an avid reader of the philosophy of history in his early days; for years he lived in "the devout hope that somewhere among them I might find the Holy Grail of sufficient explanation."[50] But he gradually abandoned the search for a single causative principle in history, and at the end of his career wrote a stinging critique on rationalist philosophy of history and utopianism.[51]

But Small left us no institute, or even an organized political opposition body of social scientists with which to counter these romantic dreams; he left us only a metaphysic of hope. As a result, philosophy of history periodically comes back into sociology, as in a large part of the work of Sorokin. Or sociology itself is equated with the philosophy of history, as in the work of Paul Barth. Albeit this is a different kind of philosophy of history—an inductive, empirical attempt to find historical laws—it is still far from the task and promise of a mature hypothetico-deductive science.

And the irony of the whole paradox that Small represents so strikingly with his thought and career is that the older "strict" sciences which he sought to appease still mock sociology in many ways. They mock it for failing while denying it the very conditions of their own success: experimentation in the external world, experimentation carried on under an agreed general theory. Some of the best social science is still considered ideology and opinion* after over a half-century of the kind of efforts that Small thought sociologists should make above everything else: teaching, public speaking, publication in massive volume, the pursuit of truth. The "other men" who would translate wisdom into action have not, needless to say, appeared. The unity that the several disciplines would bring about if left to themselves, has never been achieved.

Louis Wirth, writing a 1947 supplement to Small's 1915 overview of the history of sociology, lamented that sociology had still not found itself. It was represented by "accumulations of mountains of authentic but meaningless facts and the invention of complicated scientific gadgets for processing these crude data in a more or less mechanical fashion." This lent to sociology "a certain aura of pseudoscientific glamour . . . [but] it obviously lacked the sense of values and hence of direction of the older philosophically more sophisticated, speculative sociology, while at the same time it yielded a minimum of either practically useful or scientifically generalizable conclusions."[52]

---

* Gustav Cohn complained in 1894 that everyone who handles money imagines himself an economic theorist. The sociologist has a similar complaint: everyone who lives in society imagines himself a social theorist. But the consequences of this are grave.

One of the few things that Wirth could congratulate the discipline on was the profusion of textbooks and the forging of successful academic careers. But this, for a vision of the union of science and ethics, was the most equivocal of all. Wirth had evidently already forgotten something we noted earlier: Small's bitter caution about the "lure of profits from textbooks," "the mental pabulum" that the market digests. Small wanted a sociology that would find out "what aspects of reality most urgently demand investigation."[53] And this we have very rarely had, precisely because of the paradox it poses: it would edge sociology into a social-critical posture, since the urgent things are the current political and social events. So, with a final circular return to this problem, we are able now to conclude on Small's place in the history of social thought.*

---

* There is actually a fifth alternative in addition to the four suggested above, but it is an irregular and a terrible one to imagine, namely, that successive catastrophes caused by the divorce between mind and politics will cause men of power to turn to the social scientists for scientific guidance. The catastrophes would have to be of such magnitude that even radical advice would be followed. This answer, though terrible, is one already presented by history; it is exactly what happened to various "primitive" tribes whose culture disintegrated under Western contact. They turned to their seers to find out how much of the old ways they should abandon. At times, as in the cargo cults and revitalization movements, the change was unbelievably radical: precious wampum was thrown away, sacrosanct dogs were slaughtered, etc. The equivalent reorienting behavior to these acts in our society would be the destruction of money, bank accounts, and insurance policies, and the throwing away of our household appliances and automobiles. It is easy to see that the extent of catastrophic shock necessary for *us* to do these things is one that at present is utterly unimaginable.

5 Conclusion: The Perspective of the Present Time

When we look back over the discipline of sociology since Small began it at the turn of the century, we are left with an astonishing realization. Whatever Small's alternating misgivings, however harsh Wirth's strictures (quoted above) the discipline nonetheless succeeded in becoming what Small wanted most of all, the *objective study of social life*. We can appreciate the extent of this success by citing the most astonishing demonstration of objectivity possible for man, an objectivity that sociology achieved when it uncovered for man the *social-fictional nature of his own life-meanings*. What *Homo sapiens* needed as much as the air he breathes —the symbolically contrived meanings that keep his action moving forward and give him an imagined sense of his own worth—was revealed to him in all its social, historical, and cultural artificiality. The eighteenth century began the conquest of this last and most complex constraint on the human spirit by showing the relativity of social customs. The twentieth century completed it by showing exactly how an artificial world view became the very heart of the acting self. This is a conquest that science had to snatch almost literally from the heart of the human spirit. Little wonder that it has been building in modern times for over 200 years—from the Baron de Lahontan and his favorite Hurons to the post-Freudian psychologists.

This is actually the unraveling of the riddle of the "social forces" with which American sociology began and with which it was so plagued in its beginnings. And here again Small was right when he said in 1910 that it would take all the disciplines to converge on the central core of human conduct, and that sociology could not do it alone. Philosophy since Kant and Bentham, through Dilthey and Vaihinger, and up to Dewey's and Bentley's last work showed that man could never know absolute truth; all he could know was the response the environment gave to his own tentative symbolisms. Psychology showed that man could not be broken down into sense-data fragments, that symbols were an irreducible whole, and that man's psychological life was a totality of meanings rather than sensations.

But sociology, perhaps most clearly of all, showed a straight line of development on the problem, from Ward's attack on Spencer's mechanism and his insistence on a key place in evolution for mind, to the doctrine of the "social forces," which were interpreted as "interests" or "valuations," to the revelation in great detail and breadth of the whole web of social relations as an artificial coda that sustains society by sustaining each individual member of it. In this development the "Chicago School" had a central place. Small began it by translating and feeding Simmel into the mainstream of American sociology, thus making social forms, conventions, and "cultural games" the heart of social analysis. It was complemented by the elaboration of the social nature of the self in the self theory of Royce, Baldwin, Cooley, and Mead, which was continued by the successors of Mead at Chicago up to Erving Goffman's penetrating social psychology today.

What is Small's precise place in this development? What is his contribution to social theory? Harry Elmer Barnes, summing up his evaluation of Small, warned the reader that he was "going to risk what to many will seem a startling, if not absurd contention, namely, that in his written works, and even more in his teaching, Small's most valuable and profound doctrinal and methodological contributions were made to the fields of economics, and political science rather than to sociology. His *Adam Smith*, his *Between Eras*, his *Cameralists*, and much of his *Origins of Sociology* constitute cardinal contributions to institutional economics. If he had seen fit to put into print the well-organized material from which he gave his famous course, the "Conflict of Classes," he would have produced a work which would have made him a rival of Veblen as an original and courageous economist. His course on Karl Marx and his doctrines and influence was likewise chiefly an exercise in economic dynamics and the history of economic thought . . . Throughout most of his teaching career he gave a course under various titles which dealt with the sociological basis of the state and civic polity. There is little doubt that a half-century hence the historical student of American political theory will find much . . . of permanent value in this field in Small's writings. . . . Small is likely to have a high place in the history of functional political science in the United States." And Barnes concludes: "Finally we cannot overlook Small's contributions to ethics. . . . He powerfully promoted the movement [to identify ethics] . . . with the effort to promote a broader and more comprehensive view of social justice and human happiness."[54]

Functional political science and ethics. I have quoted Barnes's evaluation of Small at length, for two reasons: first, because it seems to me the only correct one, and second, because I want to make what may seem an even more startling and absurd contention, namely, that Small properly belongs with the two American figures who have made outstanding contributions to functional political science and ethics. Barnes mentions one—Veblen—and the other is C. Wright Mills. And here I would register my only disagreement with Barnes and say that sociology is not something different from functional political science but indeed is functional political science at its best. After all, what is it except a picture of the social system as a whole, as partly a material adaptation to the problem of survival, and partly a fiction that serves man's self-esteem according to the conventions of each society.

Veblen fused these two into a splendid picture of the workings of business and industry, and he showed that industry was the natural technical process, while business—and the behaviors that justified it—was a contrived game. Mills showed that the two were not destined to be in opposition, as Veblen thought, but that the hard material adaptation to external reality can come to be wholly submerged under the conventions of the social fiction. The result was "The Great American Celebration," social, political, economic, all in one, all inextricably interrelated, with one central thrust carrying the society forward on its ominously unreflective career. In effect, it was Veblen and Mills who gave us a view of the social reality in America that fulfilled the demands of Small's sociology.

On one level, isn't this just what Small wanted, what he insisted on time and time again as the true task of sociology—to show "the human whole," "the meanings of human experience," the reason that "men's efforts take the turn they do," when many live in society?[55] And in order to know this we had to know "human valuations and their workings," "the ways in which psychic factors work in society." Only if we know this, said Small, would social science cease to be mere knowledge, and begin "to pass over into power."[56] How would it pass into power? Because once we knew the motives of people—in their full richness and scope in any given society—we would at the same time have a clue to "the best means of promoting the development of human personality."[57] This is how the union of sociology and ethics would come about.*
Once we saw how society itself functions as a fictional convention with its roots into the very heart of the social actor, we could see

---

* Of course, if we do not want to promote the human personality, or do not believe that it is possible, then we would not be terribly concerned to understand the social system as a whole. This is the distinguishing mark of modern social research.

broadly how fictional habits cause evil in social life. This would fulfill the Enlightenment vision, which Small continued in his work.

Theoretically, there is nothing to prevent man from modifying the fictions that facilitate social living when these fictions show themselves to be constricting and defeat human adaptation and well-being. Man can begin to put the social structure itself under some degree of cognitive control. This would consummate Ward's attack on Spencer by showing how mind can cut into the determinisms of social action. Functional political science is thus an analysis of the interrelatedness of the total social system, which carries in itself an implicit critique of how it constrains man.

On another level the social theorist would have to show this constraint not only in an abstract way but in terms of concrete analysis of current events in his own social system. And it is on this level that Small's place with Veblen and Mills is even more obvious. In case there is any doubt about it, let us listen to Small's own program:

> The indicated function of social science is to be the chief organ of social self-examination. . . . [We cannot let] eighteenth-century social interpretations stand unimpeached by twentieth-century conditions. We are in danger of mistaking capitalism mitigated by patriarchalism for capitalism corrected in principle. In no period of history has it been possible for social scientists to perform more fundamentally constructive public service than present conditions throughout the world demand. To seize the opportunity we must learn how to relegate both surface phenomena and esoteric subtleties to their proportional place, and we must concentrate our forces upon radical problems.[58]

These words are almost the identical protocol for Mills's study, *The Power Elite*. We are in danger of mistaking capitalism in its guise of a broadly based, commercial industrialism as the Great American Celebration—for capitalism corrected in principle. We are in danger of overlooking the protean forms that any structure of domination can have over the human spirit unless we are willing to analyze fearlessly the social reality in its broadest relations. Today the problem of evil in human life translates itself into dimensions of the international class structure, not only the domestic one, not even principally. It translates itself into "the uncritical society," wherever it may be found, and whatever its economic forms: state socialism of Russia, world revolutionism of China, the war machine of commercial industrialism. The problem of unlimited consumer productivity dumps over into the slums of São Paulo and Caracas. The problem of maintaining internal order and unquestioning allegiance to national policy spills out of the great American, Russian, and Chinese monoliths into an international competition for power and prestige.

These are the dimensions of analysis that Small would have been comfortable with. They provide what he most wanted, a judgment of social conduct whose standard would be the effects of that conduct on the widest spectrum of humanity.[59] This is the only comprehensive view of social justice. This, and this alone, is the Enlightenment vision fulfilled in our time; it gives the possibility of a new "common view of life" that mankind can use for its own liberation. Veblen, Small, and Mills, then, group naturally together into a social-critical sociology in the service of human freedom. Nor are they alone; recently the French sociologist Gurvitch has frankly called the social sciences the sciences of human freedom. At the end of our discussion of Small's life and work we can see how far into history this definition extends. We can see that it is not only an ideal that the social sciences must strive to attain, but rather, as Small best exemplifies, the authentic tradition from which they sprung.

Are we saying that this is what sociology should be, that all research should focus only on what Small called "radical problems," that sociology should be social criticism? No, hardly that. We know how many odd and seemingly inverted kinds of scientific work it takes to know the social reality, how the idiosyncratic scholar's preoccupations one day turn out to be meaningful in a larger theoretical scheme. Above all, we are not forgetting the great historical paradox of social science, the main lesson that we have drawn from Small's career. Our omission seems to be that we have overlooked the paradox almost entirely, and this at a time when national and world events should be causing us to live more in the teeth of it than ever before. In the final analysis, only the community of scientists can decide what form their science shall take. But the lesson of Small's life is that in the social sciences today we must go back to history to find the controlling facts for these kinds of decisions; these facts do not emerge from the day-to-day disciplinary work.

If social scientists were to clarify the shape of their science, using historical bearings, perhaps we would achieve what Victor Branford called for: group consciousness of a heritage and trust around which a political party of social scientists might be formed, and which would include their supporters in other sciences and the intelligent public at large. It would advocate legislation based on the best agreed social theory.*

In the U.S. today we are able to judge the extent of the default of social scientists, who do not group themselves professionally and organizationally around certain principles and programs of

---

* To judge by recent editorials in the journals of the "hard" sciences, one could expect a considerable rally of support from the other sciences to a social-science political group. Many physical and natural scientists are literally pleading for a healing of the perennial rupture between science and society, and they know that somehow only social science can provide it.

social action. Our leaders and lawmakers consequently see no responsible scientific opposition group whose principles and programs they might want to take into account.* This failure of the sprawling organizations of social scientists to support their own best considered knowledge means that when catastrophes do come, our society will be deprived even of the recourse that primitives had. As we noted earlier, they turned to their seers for advice on which of the old ways to change and what policies to adopt. Our social scientists have gracefully avoided the only role proper to them, that of repositories of scientific wisdom in social affairs.

We can come to at least one conclusion without equivocation: a unified social science in the Enlightenment vision, or a national university in the vision of Jefferson, would have plenty of copies of Veblen's, Small's, and Mills's studies in "functional political science," and it would pass these copies around for urgent reading to government officials at all levels. And we are certainly saying that in a truly experimental democracy, as envisioned by Jefferson and his heirs up to Dewey, the legislators and executive branch would be eager to read and digest these facts, eager to study their interrelations, and eager to apply them to the ongoing formulation of law and the pursuit of social justice.

President Eisenhower's famous warning to watch out for the military-industrial complex was an intimation, however faint, of the original role of social science in government. But instead of being a fleeting afterthought to a military-diplomatic career, it would be a central preoccupation of a whole body of people in Washington, continually studying and advising on the national condition. Then we would not have to lament with Veblen that

* It is significant in this connection that a Marxist theoretician in Czechoslovakia a few years back called for an opposition party within the framework of Marxist society in order to keep Marxist doctrine healthy and growing. This was, alas, before the recent Soviet tyranny.

we know what is wrong but can do nothing, or with Mills that our best enjoinders and programs are swallowed up in silence as the nation spins on in its uncritical career.

Finally, we can say without any fear of contradiction that a society which is willing to apply social science in the active process of changing its own vested-interest institutions has never yet been seen on the face of this planet. It would be a true democracy, and it would eagerly offer its highest rewards to men like Albion Small who would radically question every single thing, except the sanctity of the individual human spirit.

II

SKETCH FOR A
CRITICAL HISTORY
OF ANTHROPOLOGY

I maintain that it is beyond dispute that anyone who has seen only one nation does not know man; he only knows those men among whom he has lived.

Everything that is done in reason should have its rules. Travel, undertaken as a part of education, should therefore have its rules. To travel for travelling's sake is to wander, to be a vagabond; to travel to learn is still too vague; learning without some definite aim is worthless. I would give a young man a personal interest in learning, and that interest, well-chosen, will also decide the nature of the instruction.
—Rousseau

Introduction

The great and good Rousseau, in the statement from *Émile* quoted on the previous page, did nothing less than lay down the task and scope of modern anthropology.

The first quotation is the mandate for modern empirical anthropological study: travel and observe; go to the remotest places, if need be, in order to learn first hand and unmistakably, the nature of man. Contemporary anthropology still holds this enjoinder dear, and although there has been some recent stirring to play down the requirement that each anthropologist "do" field work as part of his professional rite-of-passage, no anthropologist would accept anything less than the actual facts about man. In this, he has left his eighteenth-century forebears far behind.

The second quotation of Rousseau's, on the other hand, departs somewhat from our accustomed vision of the scientific quest; it enjoins us not only to learn, but to learn for a purpose, not only to travel to the ends of the earth to unravel the riddle of human nature, but to unravel it so that it is *personally* interesting to any young man.

This particular slant is hardly in the spirit of modern inductivism; it throws personal values full into the problem of science. And yet this is the distinctive Rousseau that we are rediscovering in our time. The scope of my sketch, which I will develop in the following pages, is to point out that while we have followed the first enjoinder marvelously well, we have lost sight of the second, equally vital one. The whole history of modern anthropology is, in this sense, a paradoxical one: we have carried out Rousseau's vision and betrayed it at the same time.

No critical sketch can do justice to the full dimensions of this paradox, and I see no reason to apologize for the adequacy of the one I am offering, since I claim nothing more for it than the stimulus of a sketch. We must write something for the "young man" anthropologist in the present scientific and world turmoil, else he shall never get his bearings at all; this is my reason for writing. I hope that I have been able to go to the heart of our present dilemmas and provide some kind of synthetic grasp. Perhaps, too, it will be of help to the person who will write an adequate history of social anthropology, the lack of which I. C. Jarvie has so well reminded us of in his excellent recent book, *The Revolution in Anthropology*.[1]

1   The Several Histories of Anthropology

Where in history does a science begin? Usually a science is too complex an affair for us to be able to say precisely. There is too deep a mixture of metaphysical assumptions, too wide a background of technical arts and practice, too many single contributions. All the more so with a science as broad and many-sided as the science of man. Usually we agree that the Greeks began it with their speculations on human nature, their records of foreign customs and traditions, their empirical study of man as a phenomenon in nature. But there is also wide agreement that *modern* anthropology really takes root in the Enlightenment. It was during this time that the distinctive progressive, secular, and empirical attitude that ushers in our modern epoch began. So there is really little problem of reaching general agreement, even about a science as protean as the science of man. By the time we get completely into the eighteenth century all the previous beginnings and currents become full blown and merge into the work and visions of the great names of our time—Linnaeus, Buffon, Lamarck. The problem of the history of anthropology—as A. I. Hallowell has incisively observed—is not when it began but why it has taken such a broad and rich development since the Enlightenment.[2] This is the question we want to answer.

The Science of Man as a Grand Vision

The eighteenth century was a century of great men and of grand visions, and most typical and grandest was the vision of a thoroughgoing science of man in nature, society, and history. We can say that it began with Buffon, one of the truly great men of the century, and we can understand how he stirred the hearts of men when we recall that Rousseau himself kneeled down to kiss the threshold of Buffon's house. Georges Gusdorf has called him the "new Galileo," the man who wanted to decipher the Book of Nature, rather than Holy Writ.[3] Buffon was the very model of the scientist, the "New Man" of the age. He radiated from his person the grandiose, scientific hope of the century—that man with his mind will *know* nature and with his powers will turn the whole earth to his own creative purpose.

Gusdorf, in his important historical and critical book on the science of man, has reminded us that the men who originated it were men of uncommon broadness of vision; the science to which they gave their stamp was a science of man in the fullest meaning of the term. Buffon, for example, dared to formulate a science that included the totality of nature, that would link the organic and the inorganic and place man at the terminal point in a continuous series of natural beings. His vision took in not only the earth but the origin of the planets; it took in geology before the word itself was formed; it took in paleontology and the still unborn notion of prehistory.[4] It was all there: cosmology, philosophy, natural history, the whole intelligible universe, linked in all its parts with a single chain. And it was to be hung like a wreath around the neck of man in the great celebration of the eighteenth century—the celebration of free rational man emerging from the Gothic darkness of fear, superstition, ignorance, weakness.

Of course, a chain like this had to be very thinly put together at that time. Such were the dimensions of Buffon's vision that his thought had to be premature in terms of the meagre data available at the very beginning of the modern empirical quest. There was a good deal of fancy and fable in his work, as his contemporaries were ready to point out; his view was too broad; it smacked of the cursed metaphysical systems that they sought to tear themselves away from in their careful scientific search. They were aiming to stay on the shore and gather seashells with Newton, while Buffon was trying to drink in the whole briny deep. Many admired him; many mistrusted him. Today a man like Buffon has become an impossibility; if he were to exist, our scientific Grand Inquisitor would hustle him away in the night.

This is my whole point in beginning the present sketch with Buffon as a model, and it is the same point that Gusdorf drives home. For men like Buffon, Lamarck, Saint-Hilaire, Kant—even the cautious and self-effacing Darwin who came later—anthropology was a very big thing indeed. It was nothing less than the sum total of knowledge about man. It was the science of human nature as it appears in society and history—the whole development of the human spirit out of the animal world through the dark unknown of primitive times up to the most recent gains of civilization. And all this was to be known in a new way, not fancifully, but empirically; nature would speak to us in our own experience and careful study and not in our desires and fears.

This kind of vision is surely breathtaking enough in its own right compared with the usual run of scientific ambitions today, but it is only part of the story. The best and most challenging part is yet to come (and here we must recall our second epigraph of Rousseau's). Why try to decipher this vast panorama? To what purpose? Simple curiosity and learning? Hardly. The eighteenth century wanted the biggest and clearest picture of human nature in itself and in history in order to obtain nothing less than a new moral code for the nations. The idea sounds biblical and Emersonian to us, but to the eighteenth century it was strictly within the bounds of science. We shall return later to this great and crucial problem and try to judge its relevance for our dilemmas today about the science of man.

The Dissipation of the Grand Vision

The science of man in the service of human power and freedom! Here was a grand vision that is surely unfamiliar to most of us today. Even the names of the men who held it are recalled infrequently in our graduate schools for the most part, and we read them even more rarely: Lord Kames, Lord Monboddo, Vico, Herder, Wilhelm von Humboldt, Adam Ferguson, John Millar. As the study of man developed it got away from its early sweep and promise and away from the vision of these men. In fact, the amazing thing is how quickly it happened.

Paul Topinard, in his excellent discussion of the history of anthropology published in 1885, traces the scope and varied usage of the word and fixes 1795 (the date of the third edition of Blumenbach's *De generis humani . . .*) as the date when the word "anthropology" first takes on its present usage. It is the "science of humanity."[5] At approximately the same time, in 1791, the great Immanuel Kant agreed that a voyage to discover by direct observation the original nature of man should properly be called an "anthropological expedition" (cited in Gusdorf).[6] In France, in 1803, the recently formed Society of the Observers of Man—perhaps the very first anthropological society—announced a prize to be awarded for the best study of the development of one or more infants in its interpersonal dimensions.[7] And to mention Kant again, had he not already, in his *Anthropology,* discussed the fact that the child speaks of himself in the third person before he develops a sense of himself as a subject, that he is an object of his environment before his executive ego takes shape?[8] Kant concluded that the explanation of this phenomenon poses a rather difficult task for the "anthropologist."

Decidedly, the "science of humanity" was just that at the turn of the nineteenth century. Anthropology was fully conscious of its power and scope as the study of man. In 1839 the Ethnological Society of Paris was founded; in 1842, the one in London. Toward the middle of the century the idea of prehistory emerges; collections of bones, skulls, prehistoric relics multiply; chairs of anthropology are formed in the universities. A new Society of Anthropology is formed by the encyclopedic Paul Broca in Paris in 1859, and the pressure seems to build up to an intense pitch. What was characterized as anthropology in the eighteenth century was a simple natural history approach to human and racial evolution. In 1859—the "climactic year" as Gusdorf calls it—another new dimension was added: the evolution of peoples as *societies* came into purview. Lazarus and Steinthal founded their famous *Journal of Folk-Psychology and Philology;* Bastian published his *Man in History,* and Waitz the first volume of his *Anthropology.*[9]

We might say that anthropology suddenly found itself at the

height of its vision. The new science had only to cast its olympian glance over the phenomenon of man in all its dimensions—natural, historical, social—in order to feel the thrill and power of a great new science being born. Up until about 1860 all this growth and power was in full command, perhaps best symbolized by men like Adolf Bastian, Paul Broca, Theodore Waitz. Here was the great science of man that the visionary Saint-Simon had called for, and the one that his disciple Comte had tried to systematize. But no sooner was the promised land glimpsed from the heights than the dizzying realization dawned; it began to be uncomfortably obvious that what Topinard had called the "Science of Humanity" had assumed a scope it could not continue to handle. How could the same science talk about man in nature and evolution as well as in history and society? How could it include within it disciplines like comparative psychology, sociology, medicine, abnormal psychology? It wanted to include history, too, but there was as yet no real history of masses and people, only the skewed history of great men, as Topinard himself complained.[10]

There was already too much knowledge for one science to handle comfortably. Yet look what had yet to be achieved before anthropology could even qualify as a mature synthetic science: Kant's problem of why the child develops in the third person before the first person; the problem of the origin and development of language; the differentiation of the races and its significance; the problem of folk psychology and the relation of the concepts of a whole people to the workings of the individual mind; the problem of social psychology left by Adam Smith: what holds people together in orderly functioning groups; the nature of invention, of madness; the significance of religious beliefs and rituals.

All these questions could really be understood as aspects of one: How to account for the great diversity of mankind? This was the central problem of the new science, and it was a question of such

magnitude that no sooner was it brought into some kind of comprehensive vision than the science itself was seen to be inadequate
to answer it. The result was that the grand vision of anthropology
had now to be dissipated, and it was dissipated in the two ways
that are so familiar to us.

I   THE FACILE EVOLUTIONARY SYNTHESIS

Mind can make either of two reactions to a situation as ponderous
and overwhelming as the one we traced. We might call them al-
ternately the "megalomanic" and the "fetishist" reactions. The
megalomanic reaction, if coupled with a great intelligence, actually
succeeds in making conceptual order out of the chaos of facts and
events and presents a system that is stimulating and challenging in
its economy, elegance, and order. The only drawback is that all
generalizations do violence to the individual cases, and the more
individual cases there are to be synthesized the greater the violence.
The theory of the evolution of culture was just such a synthesis;
it was an indispensible and violent ordering of the science of man
in response to the impossibility of keeping that science in some
kind of manageable form. The names here are familiar enough to
us, as well as what they tried to do.

It all began, probably, in 1760 with De Brosses and his work *Du
culte des dieux fetiches*. De Brosses showed how man progressed
from the primitive worship of fetish gods to the present high state of
civilization. This work influenced Comte and his well-known sys-
tematization of the stages of human progress. By the second half of
the nineteenth century literally a host of thinkers had their own
visions of the development of man from his primitive beginnings
on and up in a more or less universal and uniform manner to the
higher reaches of present civilization. On the way, he dropped his
various barbaric customs, his habit of half-thinking emotional
response, his false beliefs, and gradually became that epitome of

humanity that we recognize each morning in our faithful glass (if we are Western men). The familiar names of the principal thinkers who held more or less to this unilinear evolutionary schema are Spencer, Tylor, Lubbock, Frazer. There were many others, including names we have forgotten, such as John Beattie Crozier and the latter-day Comteans in England.

There is hardly any point in dwelling on this ambitious way of preserving a synthetic science of man, since we know how completely it failed. For the specialist it failed very early; for the layman it went down with the crash of World War I. In fact, World War I was a sort of empirical laboratory test case of the evolutionary hypothesis, and it was obvious that the great men were wrong, that industrialism did not bring peace, as Spencer predicted, that modern man was not more rational, as Frazer hoped. The crash was so great it threw the whole enterprise of science into doubt. Science had been linked so intimately to the idea of automatic progress that there now seemed no way to turn.[11] Many scientists turned to Freud and the unconscious to try to explain that man was swamped from the depths of nature. Hence, part of the reason for the vogue of Freud between the two World Wars. Others, devout rationalists and scientific utopians like H. G. Wells, could only die in despair.

II THE FACILE DISCIPLINARY QUEST

We noted that this vision failed very early for the specialist, and this is more to the heart of our story. It is the "fetishist" reaction to the protean problem of a science of man that has lasted up to the present day and continues to trouble us. I call it "fetishist" because it is just that: an attempt to cope with an overwhelming problem of conceptualization by biting off very tiny pieces of it and concentrating on them alone, even, to push the analogy, deriving all one's sense of self, all one's delight in life and work, from the feverish contemplation of a ludicrously limited area of reality. Of course, this does not characterize all the disciplinarians, and especially not those that we are going to talk about, but it does characterize the discipline as a whole.

Whereas the evolutionists had "lost" the science of man by mutilating it into a rigid and false mold, the disciplinarians lost it by dispersing and obscuring its central problem—how to account for the diversity of mankind from the supposedly similar workings of the human psyche everywhere? And as we know so well, or should know, a science without an identifiable central problem is hardly a science at all. In 1860 the disciplines had already begun their great proliferation and concentration on precise problems on very circumscribed areas. By 1880 the diversity was extreme. Perhaps the new tone of the times is best symbolized by what happened to the great Comtean journal, *La Philosophie positive,* founded at Comte's death to carry on his synthetic ambitions. It folded in 1883 after a mere fifteen years of publication. On the occasion of its demise Wyrouboff lamented the reason: there was a decline of interest in general, synthetic questions. Instead, the attention of all was on the details of the practical business of everyday life. At approximately the same time in the United States the great hope of the American Social Science Association—keeping all social knowledge focused on social reconstruction—began its long and continuing death as the various disciplines—political science, economics, history, sociology—pulled away from the Association's sponsorship. There was no longer to be any general science of man; that was the obvious message of the *Zeitgeist.*

The Attack

The richest part of our story is what took place in anthropology, principally in the United States, from the date of the founding of the Bureau of Ethnography in Washington in 1879. Anthropology became professional and scientific in full measure, and it did so by reacting against Tylor and the unilinear evolutionists. I have called this the "facile" disciplinary quest, and I use the word advisedly. If the evolutionists were facile in their hope of fitting all the new facts of the science of man into one neatly progressive framework, then their adversaries had, in a way, an even more facile time attacking them. It was a real old-fashioned free-for-all, punching holes in the armchair theories of the older generation of stay-at-home theorists. Undoubtedly, the new men worked harder, going out and studying firsthand and often under very difficult, unpleasant, and even hazardous conditions. They were entitled to a self-satisfied and condescending use of the facts they had so painfully and personally culled. But the use of these facts to puncture the older theory was child's play.

The evolutionists assumed that the same phenomena were always due to the same causes, so they looked over the totality of human cultures, and by comparing like phenomena, tried to reduce them all to similar types and classes. What emerged was a uniform pattern of cultural evolution in all human groups. They were not really doing "historical" evolutionism but rather using a methodology proper to the objects of natural science, as Redfield has pointed out.[12] Thus, while they thought they were using the fruitful scientific comparative method, they were actually doing it the utmost violence by taking facts out of their own unique historical context and falsely lumping them together with other facts which they resembled.

When Boas, Lowie, Kroeber, Sapir, and Goldenweiser brought this misuse of method under attack, they had an easy time of it. Since all they had to do was to adduce evidence of a single case that did not conform to the generalizations of the evolutionists. It was really a matter of simply saying "In tribe 'X' this is not the way it is." And this could be applied to any of the neat uniformities that the evolutionists had put forth with such finality, e.g., that there were stages in the evolution of the family, that the bilateral family is a late cultural development, that there is a fixed succession of maternal and paternal descent, that historically matriarchy preceded patriarchy, that each culture had to pass through stages in the development of tools and weapons from stone to copper to iron, that each had to pass through the domestication of animals, the manufacture of pottery, or else it was doomed to be classified on a "lower" plane of evolutionary development, that kinship bonds precede territorial bonds historically, that preanimism or "animatism" is the earliest stage of religion, preceding animism, that totemism is combined with the idea of mana, etc., etc., etc. The list is very long, and the minute record is there for any serious student to see.

It will also be very plain how satisfied these people were with their talent and penchant for demolition; this is very clear in someone like Lowie. In fact, the analytic destructiveness of his attack is very Voltairean and smacks of the spirit of the earlier skeptical analysis of the eighteenth century. In his well-known book *Are We Civilized?* Lowie even argued that we are not more civilized than those we term primitive. It was the old eighteenth-century debate between the *ferini* and *anti-ferini* over again, and for similar reasons: to attack the self-satisfied picture we had created of the process of evolution with ourselves at its terminus.

Let us hasten not to give the wrong impression. This process of analytic breakdown was not destructive in intent; it was animated by the urge to real scientific clarification. The problem that Boasian anthropology had to clarify was the real and central one of anthropology, and these men were not shirking it. The problem was, as we said: How did things get to be as they are in the vast panorama of human groups? The evolutionists had argued that the same things were due to the same causes, because man's mind is everywhere basically the same. Bastian, for example, saw the human mind as reducible to "elementary thoughts," which always acted alike; his reason for tracking down the primitive was to try to see the elementary thoughts in pure culture. This was a curious form of philosophic rationalism combined with natural science method; Boas saw it as a kind of mysticism. Others argued that the human panorama could best be explained as a result of diffusion or borrowing of ideas, rather than independent development of each culture. It is this argument that Boas and his followers wanted to settle scientifically. There was only one way, and that was by a new historical-empirical method. In Boas's own words:

> However this controversy may be settled, it is clear that it must lead to detailed historical investigations, by means of which definite problems may be solved, and that it will furthermore lead to psychological researches into the conditions of transmission, adaptation, and inventions. Thus this controversy will carry us beyond the limits set by the theory of elementary ideas, and by that of a single system of the evolution of civilization.[13]

In other words, each culture would have to be understood in its own historical growth, and only by comparing the histories of each growth could valid general evolutionary sequences be found. The symbol for this new approach was Boas's well-known reorganization of museum exhibits, in which he grouped artifacts together by tribe and area and not, as was formerly done, grouping like objects with like, no matter what culture they came from. This was the "functionalism" basic to any mature science, which Malinowski later laid claim to. The point about Boasian anthropology was that it had no vested interest, since it was still focused on the large central question with which the science of man began. Thus Boas was, as Herskovits reminded us, historicist, diffusionist, evolutionist, functionalist, psychologist. He was "all" these things, because he saw culture as dynamic and understandable only in the broadest possible interrelated way.[14]

There is no need to dwell here on the success of Boas's reorientation of anthropology. The literature is there for all to see: the rich collection of monographs, the careful record of fact, the neat puncturing, as we said, of armchair theory, the establishment of a respected and truly scientific discipline, numbering literally thousands of workers and teachers. It is all secure. And yet the full story is not told. The victory of the new anthropology was purchased at an enormous price, and it is only recently (if we leave aside the stirring of someone like Redfield) that some anthropologists have begun to clamor that the price was too great, that anthropology in its very success had lost its soul. Let us sketch in some of the background of this lament before we give it full ear.

The Paradoxical Outcome of the Victory

The triumph of Boasian anthropology ushered in a long period of what we might call methodological discomfort. And as Whitehead has cautioned us, when a science begins to bog down in a fixation on method, it is a sure sign that something more ominous is under way. For one thing, there was a complete revulsion against all kind of historical method, perhaps best represented by Malinowski and Radcliffe-Brown. Malinowski's "new" functionalism was a reaction *in toto* against Frazer and Tylor. It was a British counterpart to the American reorientation, and it stressed field work against speculation, careful study of each individual culture in its own context against uncritical use of a blanket comparative method. Radcliffe-Brown pushed the idea even further by stressing "structure-functionalism." He meant to show that the structure of each society has its own dictates and may even work against human needs; structures have to be analyzed on their own level.

The new fixation on structural-functional method succeeded in obscuring the historicity of cultures. Everything came to focus on the "working together" of things, of the elements of each particular culture. With the slighting of the perspective of history and the focus on the workings of things in the present, anthropology gradually lost sight of its own historical mandate, of its grounding in values, and of its high ambition as a synthetic science of man.

This is perhaps best seen not in England but in the very place where Boasian anthropology had triumphed. The new accent on empirical history, ushered in by Boas, quickly lapsed into an American brand of strict functionalism called Culture and Personality, or psychological anthropology. It was a logical, even apodictic outcome of Boas's own vision. Had he not told us that the main thing was not to reconstruct the stages of culture but rather to determine the "*processes* by which certain stages of culture have developed"? We are not interested, said Boas, in customs and beliefs as such. "We desire to learn the reasons why such customs and beliefs exist." And in 1920 he summed up the problem of the new anthropology in these words:

> The activities of the individual are determined to a great extent by his social environment, but in turn his own activities influence the society in which he lives, and may bring about modifications of its form. . . . [We are interested] in the question of the way in which the individual reacts to his whole social environment, and to the differences of opinion and of modes of action that occur in primitive society and which are the cause of far-reaching changes."[15]

On the face of it, this new orientation was innocent enough of any intent to scuttle the study of historical process, and certainly at that stage of the development of anthropology a close scrutiny of the problem of the individual in relation to society was more than necessary. Durkheim had not really clarified what he promised;

he had not shown exactly how the individual is fashioned by the social group. And Freud, with his false sexual and instinct theory and his wild and shabby historical speculations, was someone who had to be lived through, digested, and overcome. There was a need to see exactly how the individual and society were related in terms of the various milieus of ideas into which individuals were born and in terms of the different talents, inventiveness, energy, "subjectivity" of the individuals who compose the society.

But the outcome of Culture and Personality delivered less than the promise. As K. O. L. Burridge has recently warned, Culture and Personality seems very near to its end without having fulfilled its ambition. It had promised, especially in the work of Ruth Benedict, to elucidate the union of individual psychology and culture. But although it gave us a deeper knowledge of psychology, says Burridge, it did not give us an adequate knowledge of culture. We still lack a general theoretical union of social institutions and individual psychology, and our problem is still how to get a synthetic framework that unites the two into "some meaningful and fruitful relationship."[16] There is no doubt that Burridge's complaint is well taken, and we shall see further on the real gravamen of his critique.

What is obvious is that functionalism of any variety, either structural or psychological, has failed to give us the "complete" picture of the workings of each culture, as Boas had hoped. And we should not be astonished since "science," almost by definition, means "incomplete" picture. And so, by focusing on the narrow area of the processes of individual and social transactions, something very large indeed was lost, namely the larger historical panorama that the closer study had intended to clarify. The new method was thus a kind of unintended "fetishization" of the field of anthropology, which could not have been otherwise. Commenting on Boas's words (quoted above), Herskovits says:

This [study of the individual reacting to society] ... was anything but simple where the actual processes of change could not be observed, and historical relationships could only be reconstructed. This is why, by the logic of the problem, anthropology came to study culture change in process or, as it is called, acculturation.[17]

It is very clear to us now that by the same apodictic logic the *psychological* study of acculturation had to obscure and oust the historical one. One was scientific, the other speculative and reconstructionist. Once we focused on the present and the observable the larger historical problems of anthropology had to go by the board.

The whole recent stirring over historical methodology, largely undertaken by Evans-Pritchard, is an indication of this dissatisfaction. Evans-Pritchard understands that anthropology lost something and that it can get it back again only by forging its links with history. He wants to get anthropology back to where it was at the turn of the century, and he cites with approval Maitland's famous dictum that anthropology must choose between becoming history or nothing. What is anthropology? asks Evans-Pritchard. It is not the positivist discipline that sprang from the Enlightenment and tried to model itself on the natural sciences by seeing societies as natural systems and by understanding man as an automaton subject to regular sociological laws. With this kind of ambition the anthropologist was led to turn his back on history, because it did not give him the kind of rigid laws that he wanted in order to plan and predict human behavior.

Instead, says Evans-Pritchard, anthropology is an historical type of study, which sees societies as systems only because social life must have patterns of some kind, and man as a reasonable creature always gives it more or less intelligible patterns. Anthropology tries to see things in pattern, and comparatively, as well as in their underlying dynamics. And it does this in order to understand man and his variations in society and history. The aim of this kind of anthropology is not to give fundamental laws leading to prediction and planning, which is what the positivist wanted and still wants. Rather, it would give a record, based on the closest empirical work, for other sciences to use. With this kind of anthropology there need be no argument about a one-and-only method; it could be synchronic and diachronic, as need be, in order to give the fullest possible picture of each society.[18]

In Evans-Pritchard's program—which he repeated in a talk[19] a decade after this enjoinder was made—we recognize, in effect, Boas himself, and as we shall see further on, Lowie too. But almost a half-century had passed, and the program of Boas and Lowie had not been fulfilled. We are entitled to feel, somewhat uncomfortably, that this new discussion of old method, is itself a *non sequitur* for the failure of the Boasian vision.

This is nowhere more clear than when we examine the dilemmas of a broad and sensitive thinker like Robert Redfield, who was very much concerned about what anthropology was and what it was for. In a very early paper he tried to reconcile the historical and natural-science approaches of anthropology, and he had to conclude that it was a historical science that "ever and again tends to become a natural science."[20] In other words, anthropology was an historical study that tends to focus on repetitions and regularities. But in a very late paper the confusion of method remains, and Redfield cites it as a continuing source of ambiguity. It "is one of the disturbing and stimulating aspects of anthropology."[21] How to wish it away, except to conclude, as Boas and Evans-Pritchard do, that there is no real clash of method, that what anthropology wants is to see things in their maximum togetherness, and for this, all methods merge.

Yet Redfield does not lay aside his perplexity easily. This long and late review article on the nature of anthropology is worth our careful and close attention, so let us follow Redfield's reasoning a little further. In a section titled "Anthropology as 'Freedom in Tension' " he says:

> One might speak of anthropology as enjoying and also as suffering from the . . . polarities and ambiguities of its subject matter and its method. . . . Anthropology is thus provocatively undecided as to whether its subject matter is mankind *in toto* or man as a cultural being. . . . It is unclear as to whether it moves toward the writing of a science (or perhaps separable sciences of social relations and of culture) or toward the writing of histories. [Anthropology is comfortable with Radin's impressionism, with the study of rats, neuroses, Burckhardt, Santayana, Breasted.][22]

These are words that scarcely reflect a science in command of itself. It is more like chaos. Redfield seems to know this, because he continues in a similar pleading manner: "Experiencing such pulls toward disintegration, anthropology remains integrated by a number of centripetal forces [e.g., the commitment by all to objectivity; the study of the unity of society; the focus on mankind as a lifeform; on ecology with its own special unifying effect, and so on.]" This is hardly an imposing list of powerful centripetal forces; they would never pass muster as true synthesizing principles that a science needs. It is no surprise, then, to read the final things that hold the chaotic multiplicity of anthropology together, in Redfield's view. They are nothing else than its established university chairs, its association, and the fact that it is *a society* itself.[23]

This is a pitiful pleading of a case by someone of Redfield's unusual acumen. It is evident that he is not comfortable, and we know why from the corpus of his writings. The flourishing disciplinary professionalism in the service of strict science is not all that the generous humanitarian thinker had in mind. He wanted a science of man *for* man, for human freedom, for the community of mankind.

It is only when we get to the close of his long essay that we catch a glimpse of his real intent; here he says that anthropology in its relationships to the humanities comes into contact with philosophy, and here it meets the realm of value. The realm of value is part of man's engagement in life as man, as shaper and creator, and not as mere disinterested scholar. And this leads us naturally to something new and different. Redfield's essay ends abruptly on the following note: "The conception of anthropology as a purely theoretical part of natural history is now qualified by the recognition of applied anthropology, of 'action anthropology' . . . In advising men of action . . . anthropologists come to entertain the question: What, then, is the good life?"[24]

So that was it after all! After all its twisting and torturings, all its branches and method, all its ambiguity and tension, and satisfaction in that very tension—anthropology was fortunate to find its relation to the other humanities and its outlet in applied anthropology. It is here that the puzzled question can occur as an afterthought, as a belated discovery, a new dawning realization when brought face-to-face with the need to do a job for government, or for business, as a musing in the company tent at night under the mosquito net: "What, after all, is the good life?"

I have burdened the reader with this discourse on Redfield's important evaluation of professional anthropology (it was undertaken for the major appraisal in 1953 of *Anthropology Today*) only to be able to better bring out what we might well say is the "cumulative ineffectuality" of his discussion. The point is that even Redfield could only make anthropology meaningful by a sort of sleight-of-hand, pendant afterthought on how it relates to human value. It is pathetic that someone of his uniqueness and stature should have to be almost wily about the true end and aim of anthropology. Yet the shocking fact is that "What is the good life?" is the great question of Enlightenment science, of the whole eighteenth century. It is the unique and absolute predication for modern anthropology; it is the first thought of social science—as we shall see in Part II—now offered as an afterthought by one of our most characteristic modern Enlightenment thinkers. There seems to be no better way to sum up the paradox of the victory of Boasian anthropology: unilinear evolutionism was wholly discredited, by a discipline that became superbly scientific and professional. Only now, the unifying thinker, the moralist and humanist, finds himself straining against this very creation.

The Real Problem

This, then, was the real problem, obscured by all the discussion about method: whether anthropology is a nomothetic or an idiographic science; whether it is a synchronic or a diachronic study; whether it is history or natural science; whether it only seems like natural science, partly because prehistory offers no documents, and so on, and on. The real problem underneath all this is what on earth anthropology is all about. What happened, to be blunt, to the science of man? What do all these "human scientists" in our universities represent? The methodological disputes, earnest as they were and clarifying as they proved to be, only obscured the fact that something more ominous was afoot, namely, the loss of the science of man itself. Today we can see all this very clearly, perhaps for the first time. From the failure of Boasian anthropology and from the new stirring toward history and synthesis a deeper realization has been born: modern anthropology is an eminently successful science, but it no longer knows itself.

No wonder we have recently seen a few of the sharpest and most

sweeping condemnations ever pronounced on a thriving science. I
am thinking of Gusdorf's broad-ranging and scholarly critique and
I. C. Jarvie's—both cited earlier. Gusdorf, having carefully traced
the history of anthropology from Buffon through the nineteenth
century, noted the ominous turn that took place around 1860. It
was then that the new science surveyed the magnitude of its task
of understanding man and began its luxuriant disciplinary proliferation. Gusdorf's lament over the modern condition of anthropology is uncompromising in its pessimism: "Anthropology
is becoming more and more of an exact science, but we know less
and less exactly about what. In any case, the multiplicity of anthropologists is the best proof—if not the only one—of the existence of anthropology."[25] Had not Redfield said something similar
but from an optimistic, professional point of view? For Gusdorf
anthropology was once a science of man, centered on man, like
the Encyclopedia of the eighteenth century that gave it birth. Now,
laments Gusdorf, the center of anthropology is everywhere, and
its circumference nowhere; and he cites with approval Teilhard
de Chardin's similar complaint: "In our age of Science, we have
still not been able to stake out a Science of Man."[26] And Gusdorf
closes his probing review of the problem, with this challenge: "The
question is to find out whether the very word anthropology still
has any meaning, and if it has, what that meaning might be."[27]

Summary and Conclusion:
The Key to the Paradoxical Outcome

What I have tried to do in the preceding few pages is to present
a rough sketch of the beginnings and the modern outcome of anthropology to remind the reader that there were larger problems
and a broader vision, which were lost, and to quote a few authorita-

tive voices in a direct or indirect lament over the disciplinary outcome. But in presenting such an argument it is always helpful if
one can pinpoint more or less exactly what went wrong, and where.
The key to the paradoxical outcome of anthropology, if there is
any key, would most likely be found in the thoughts and careers
of the people who were most instrumental in making it into a
successful discipline. Let us, then, look first at Franz Boas.

Boas is the one who practically single-handed fashioned a successful academic discipline of anthropology in America, and helped
make a respectable exact science of what was previously a mass of
speculation and good intention. In this he reminds one very much
of his counterpart in sociology—Albion Small, whom we discussed
in the previous essay. We saw how Small achieved the scientific
respectability he sought but only at the price of abandoning the
social problem and the ethical promise of social science. Now,
when we turn to anthropology, we can see a similar outcome in
the career of Boas and of his disciple Lowie. The same thing happened in England in the career of Malinowski, and it persists despite the critique of antihistorical method by Evans-Pritchard. It
also seems to be represented in France somewhat belatedly, in the
career of Lévi-Strauss. Let us then turn to Boas and see the striking
analogies between him and Small.

We can expect to get the best insights into the history of a
discipline if we study the reading of it by one of the scientists who
made the biggest advances in it. Also, we can see with extreme
clarity just what that scientist's vision of his own discipline is. This
is nowhere more clear than in Boas's critically important paper on
the history of anthropology, which he prepared for the International Congress of Arts and Science at St. Louis in 1904. In it we
have the picture of a man fully conscious of the ethical significance
of his science, fully cognizant of the large problems that his discipline addresses itself to, recognizing its superordinate, general-

izing nature, and yet, at the very same time, fully intent on forging
a precise and respectable science, a science that would not frighten
others with the bogey of academic imperialism, a science that would
be fully acceptable as a peer member of the community. Let us look
somewhat closer at this paradoxical position of Boas.

In the first place, what began as a superordinate, generalizing
science gave way in his thinking to a *method* and to an *attitude*.
This is very clear in his praise of Herder, Spencer, and Tylor,
[who were] responsible for the "very existence" of anthropology.
Without their evolutionary schema, how could we ever have ordered the "chaos of facts"? We needed a "firm hand," and their
bold generalizations provided it. Did this, then, in Boas's view, set
up anthropology as the general evolutionary science of man, the
co-ordinating vision of Saint-Simon, Condorcet, Herder, Kant,
Comte? Hardly. No sooner had he given credit to the evolutionists
for making sense out of chaos than he demotes anthropology to
the status of just another discipline:

> The *general* problem of the evolution of mankind is being
> taken up now by the investigator of primitive tribes, now by
> the student of the history of civilization. We may still recognize
> in it the ultimate aim of anthropology in the wider sense of the
> term, but we must understand that it will be reached by co-
> operation between all the mental sciences and the efforts of the
> anthropologist.[28]

In other words, the ultimate generalizing aim of anthropology is
no longer the aim of anthropology alone, but of all the mental
(social) sciences together. This is an answer to the rash imperialism
of the older time, which was still being echoed in anthropology:

> Conscious of the invigorating influence of our point of view
> and of the grandeur of a single all-compassing science of man,

enthusiastic anthropologists may proclaim the mastery of anthropology over older sciences that have achieved where we are still struggling with methods, that have built up noble structures where chaos reigns with us, the trend of development points in another direction, in the continuance of each science by itself, assisted where may be by anthropological methods. . . .[29]

It is almost as though Albion Small were speaking in an adjoining room, and we could hear his echo through the wall. Anthropology (sociology) has no business lording it over the older disciplines in an imperialistic, superordinate pose; the older disciplines have built up sound method, real scientific stature, which we anthropologists (sociologists) must now strive to equal, if we are to be respected and accepted. The one thing that anthropology (sociology) has to offer the older disciplines is a unique method or attitude, which will help them to invigorate their data. *This* is our contribution. What Herder, Spencer, and Tylor really achieved that was of lasting value, in Boas's words, was not a science of man but rather an attitude of historical, genetic inquiry, which "sowed the seed of the anthropological spirit in the minds of historians and philosophers." As he says, anthropology had hardly taken shape as a science when it "became a method applicable to all the mental sciences, and indispensable to all of them."[30] That is to say, anthropology had hardly taken shape as a science when it abandoned its vision and became a method that anyone could use and that would be parceled out to the other disciplines. I see no other way of reading what Boas means.

As for anthropology itself, even when it is down to size as a peer discipline where chaos still reigns (actually, then, less than a peer), it will have to retrench even further:

The field of research that has been left for anthropology in the narrower sense of the term is, even as it is, almost too wide, and there are indications of its breaking up [i.e., linguistics and biology are breaking off, rightly, into separate sciences, and anthropology will thus probably one day be characterized by the study of primitive customs and beliefs only]. Nevertheless, we must always demand that the anthropologist who carries on field-research must be familiar with the principles of these three methods, since all of them are needed for the investigation of his problems. No less must we demand that he had a firm grasp on the general results of the anthropological method as applied by the various sciences.[31]

And why must the new anthropologist have this firm grasp? Because "it alone will give his work that historic perceptive which constitutes its higher scientific value."[32]

No comment is really necessary; anthropology has gone the gamut from a synthetic science of man to a "perspective" or an attitude. Yes, we can realize, and sympathize with Boas, that anthropology did so under the impress of scientific competition and the weight of its own vast empirical data. But, as Gusdorf lamented, when it did this it had to become more and more exact while knowing less and less exactly about what. The central evolutionary schema was lost, and with it, the synthetic science centered on man.

Like Albion Small, Boas had to lament the fact that since anthropology had been reduced to a perspective for specialists there was nothing to guarantee that the perspective would continue to characterize anthropologists themselves. Speaking of the anthropology of that time, Boas lamented that the student's work is directed principally from personal love of the question he poses and his desire to clarify it, rather than from the necessary scientific awareness of where his special problem fits in the general theoretical discussions that make a science. "It must be said with regret that the number of anthropological observers who have a sufficient understanding of the problems of the day is small."[33] In his very last contribution, a few months before his death, Boas echoed this warning: anthropology was succeeding, but it was in danger of forgetting what it started out to learn. Again we can note the remarkable similarity to Small's lifelong discomfort over a discipline that became a scientific success. In Boas's words:

> Reviewing the development of anthropology as a whole I think we may rejoice in the many new lines of research that have been taken up. . . . There is perhaps some danger that, engrossed in the difficult psychological problems involved in the analysis of culture, we may forget the importance of the general historical problem with which our science started, but I am certain that with the broadening of our view the varied approaches to an understanding of the history of mankind will be harmoniously elaborated and lead us to a better understanding of our own society.[34]

Herskovits ended his book about Boas on this hopeful note, but as we saw earlier in Burridge's lament, the "difficult psychological problems" of Culture and Personality have not led us to the harmoniously elaborated view of the individual and society that it promised. Instead, Culture and Personality research has borne out Boas's fear that the specialized student would forget the larger historical problems and find no place in which to fit his work, other than the proper Rorschach blot or computer slot.

In one final way Boas kept the integrity of the early vision of anthropology, and in this too he resembled Small. This was his awareness of the ethical function of his science. Whatever else anthropology might be, it had primary value as education—as liberal or *liberating* education, in the original Rousseauian sense. Boas says:

> Of greater educational importance is its power to make us understand the roots from which our civilization has sprung,

to impress us with the relative value of all forms of culture, and
thus to serve as a check to an exaggerated valuation of the stand-
point of our own period, which we are only too liable to consider
the ultimate goal of human evolution. . . .[35]

Obviously Boas has one eye, as always, on the unilinear evolutionists, but just as obviously he means what he says. The use of
anthropology in life as a corrective for false beliefs and social
shibboleths runs all through his work. And, as George Stocking
has shown in a fine critical-historical paper,[36] it was with Boas
that the concept of culture was transmuted from its earlier evolutionist usage. Instead of connoting that higher degree of civilization
which was progressively freeing man from barbarism, it connoted
instead the burden of social learning in any society, the oppressive
weight of tradition. Today it may seem strange to many of us to
hear the anthropologist call tradition to account. One might have
expected Boas at least to laud the primitive life ways. But he was
no dreamy romanticist, and in his personal credo he stated that the
task of man everywhere was to fight the shackles in which tradition holds him. In this, he was kin to Marx, who talked of tradition
as a great pyramid weighing on man's brain; he was also kin to
Rousseau, as we said, but without Rousseau's uncritical attitude
toward the primitive. Boas had learned the full scientific lesson
from social life.

In all this, then, Boas was a pivotal figure, and in all this he
resembled Albion Small. His vision for anthropology was ambiguous. It kept the larger problems in focus even while pursuing
the most minute research; it kept its historical perspective even
while doing non-historical studies; it shrank to the size of a single,
sister discipline in the social sciences, and yet it kept the broad
ethical imperative of a science designed to promote the human
spirit. Alas, there was no way to guarantee that the successors of
Boas could live with this many-faceted ambiguity, and the subse-

quent history of anthropology, like sociology, was a history in which the challenge and the tensions of the ambiguities were effaced.

This is nowhere more patent than in Boas's student, Robert Lowie. With Lowie anthropology became the strictest possible discipline and at the same time degenerated into an almost pure positivism. It was with Lowie that cultural relativism lost its critical cutting edge—that the purpose of anthropology became that of furthering itself as a discipline. I do not mean to implicate Lowie "personally" in this judgment; the fact is that the descendants of Boas were almost forced into their vision of science by the rigorous mandate for fancy-free empirical work that Boas passed on to them. It could have been someone other than Lowie, just as in sociology it could have been anyone after Small, given the climate for research that Small created at Chicago. Lowie's stature as a scientist is beyond question, and he would have been the first to welcome scientific clarification. He was second to none in pressing home the decisive attack, in finding the root fallacy of another's thought. Well, the root fallacy of Lowie's vision of ethnography was that it carried over all the positivist trends of Boas's work to their ineluctable conclusion.

What characterized anthropology, in Lowie's view? For one thing, the elimination of value judgments; values are natural phenomena to be studied. Yes, we can even study the Nazis as objects. With complete cultural relativism even the relative malevolence of cultures "simply [does] not enter" into our formulations.[37]

And what about the urge for a synthetic or "complete theory" of human behavior, the original mandate of the science of man? Lowie answers—and I must quote him in full, for it is very revealing:

If it holds true generally that no branch of learning is under obligation to ape the procedures of any other, this may be as-

serted most emphatically with reference to the search for ultimate explanations. For that reason it strikes me as a momentary
relapse into unwarranted subservience to an older discipline
when Professors Kroeber and Kluckhohn in their recent treatise
on *Culture* wistfully contrast the theory of gravitation with the
lack of a "full theory of culture" and declare that "we have
plenty of definitions but too little theory." Certainly we have too
little *sound* theory, but I doubt whether even physics can boast
of a complete theory; and because cultural phenomena are in-
comparably more complex than those of physics, because they
have come to be studied at a much later period, it seems unrea-
sonable to expect the same measure of integration either now or
in the future. As Thurnwald aptly contends, the web of socio-
cultural phenomena is too intricate to permit a resolution into
all its components without residue, yet we must attempt to discover all possible connections and determinants.[38]

There it is, the positivism in pure dosage. It is as easy—and
almost as embarrassing—to punch holes in this kind of positivism
as it was for Lowie to demolish the evolutionists. To take him
at his own words, if anthropology is under no obligation to ape
any other science, then why the confident comparison of anthropology with physics as a model of theoretical explanation? Besides,
no science can boast of a complete theory; there is simply no such
thing. Furthermore, what makes the study of culture, which began
with Herodotus, as Lowie himself says, such a late development in
comparison with physics? And isn't Herodotus' firsthand observation preferable to Democritus' armchair theorizing? And, finally,
how can a scientist confidently write off the degree of future advance of his science? Has any science ever been able, and can
any science ever hope, to resolve all its components without residue? It is all simply incredible.

What we would expect of this kind of scientific orientation is the building of a discipline by focusing on an infinitude of narrow areas. And if we want to be truly "daring," then, like Merton in sociology, we would try to aim for theories "of the middle range." Thus Lowie outlines the program for ethnology:

> None of these writers [Morgan, Schmidt, Childe, Steward, Tylor, Radcliffe-Brown, Murdock, Lévi-Strauss, Eggan] would claim to have found a full theory of social structure, but as Eggan remarks: "Generalizations do not have to be universal in order to be useful." In the processual sphere [i.e., functional regularities] the progress of ethnography lies in the ever-increasing and increasingly better-founded determination of functional relationships between descriptively isolable elements —in other words, in constantly detecting more and more organic bonds between apparently disparate phenomena. A single formula for the cultural universe, a simple solution of its enigmas, would prove a snare and a delusion. On the historical side, ethnography has assiduously determined an infinitude of special intertribal relationships and sequences. In broad outline, at least, the main steps have been traced by which the more complex civilizations of the Old and the New Worlds, respectively, have been built out of simpler beginnings. The whole story will never be known, but every synthesis of field discoveries with archaeological research marks another step in the scientific progress of the discipline.[39]

On the face of it, Lowie has here kept the broader historical-evolutionary interest; but this is only an appearance. Since the whole story will never be known, the purpose of anthropology is to keep filling it in. Generalizations do not have to be universal; they merely have to be useful—useful to the progress of the discipline. The purpose of anthropology has become solely self-furthering.

But what about the broad outline of the main steps by which

civilization developed? If this has been achieved, has not the purpose of anthropology been largely fulfilled? Or *is* this the purpose
of anthropology? Does this solve the great and central problem of
early anthropology, namely, the problem of how the diversity of
mankind grew out of a general psychic sameness? This is the
burning question, as we shall see in Part II of our essay. But already we know that the broad outline of social development, as
traced by anthropology, does not solve this problem, because it
has not fulfilled the task that Boas laid out, namely, to discover
the processes of cultural change in both individuals and societies.
We still do not have a general theory of the interrelationships of
man and society in social history. We have to know the causes of
how things came to be as they are; we have to know why things
happened as they did, and why we are where we are today.

Lowie was not shirking this task. The simple matter seems
to be that he was confused rather than unwilling to face the earlier
challenge of anthropology. The dilemma of the new scientific discipline grew out of the very search for scientific respectability on
the disciplinary model. Nowhere is this more clear than in Lowie's
attempt to come to grips with what ethnology is. Here we see the
basic contradiction between his definition of ethnography as a discipline and of its subject matter or what it proposes to study. What
is ethnology?

> Ethnology is simply science grappling with the phenomena
> segregated from the remainder of the universe as 'cultural'. It is
> a wholly objective discipline, whether it deals with subjective
> attitudes or not . . . and by the demonstration of functional rela-
> tionships it may attain to the degree of generalization consistent
> with its own section of the universe.[40]

This is the narrowing down of the discipline to a "section of the
universe" that Boas had passed on, and on the face of it, it seems

logical enough. Lowie was eminently a scientist, and he knew that even this new and restricted discipline must have a larger problem, a central aim. What would be the central aim of a new specialized discipline? It would have to be something manageable, says Lowie, something that could be "delimited" and "rigorously circumscribed,"[41] else how could anthropology take its place as a peer and sister discipline?

This new central aim and problem of the discipline of anthropology would be the concept of culture,

> variously adumbrated, but not clearly envisaged before Klemm, and not rigorously circumscribed before Tylor's classic definition in 1871. Then at last it became obvious that culture embraced everything transmitted . . . by membership in a social group. . . . This totality could no longer be adequately studied by the way, but required a specialist's concentration. As a matter of fact, if a geographer or a biologist could not do justice to the whole range of these phenomena, neither could an ethnographer. It developed that the aims of science could be best served by further specialization and that certain phases of culture could be adequately investigated only through collaboration . . . the ethnographer deals with the total range of human activity as socially determined. . . .[42]

I have quoted Lowie again at length to show how deeply the confusion that Boas passed on to his successors went. Culture was "the total range of human activity as socially determined." This was the province of the ethnographer; he had finally found something that could be "rigorously circumscribed" and handled by a "specialist's concentration." But no, says Lowie, even then culture is too vast to be studied by any specialist. Therefore, the ethnographer must share his specialty with other collaborators.

What are we to make of all this? Ethnography found something that could be rigorously circumscribed, therefore it attained the stature of a science with its own special central problem. On the other hand, its specialty could not be rigorously circumscribed but had to be parceled out to others. From this we must conclude that ethnography did not have any claim to being a special science. It was a discipline that could not handle its central problem, *ergo,* a discipline that had no right to exist as a separate science. Yet it did study something, some special area of the world of culture, and this was the area of primitive beliefs and customs, as Boas had foreseen. But this study did not serve to illuminate any central problem, since anthropology could not handle its central problem but had given it over to the other disciplines to share. And so what was lost was precisely the "why" of the science of anthropology; it existed only to feed on its special area of subject matter. In the anthropology of Boas's successors the reason for studying culture had been forgotten, as Boas feared it would be.*

Boas hoped that ethnography could at least claim a special attitude, the empirical, historical, genetic attitude that would also be adopted by the other sciences. But as we have seen in discussing Evans-Pritchard's recent essays on methodology, it was precisely this attitude that was lost. The once-proud science of man no longer had anything to characterize it. In becoming a sister discipline without any central problem peculiar to it, the only relevance it could hope to attain was to be a "helping discipline," providing data on primitive life, or on certain other areas of the cultural world that show functional interconnections. We noted earlier that this is

---

* Paul Radin is perhaps the outstanding exception to this *dénouement* of Boasian anthropology. See Arthur J. Vidich's probing and provocative essay on Radin's place in the crisis of ethnological theory;[43] it is an important document in the present reappraisal, and should be read alongside this sketch. The next task for students is to evaluate, in turn, Radin's search for an "essential human nature" along inverted Jungian lines.

what Evans-Pritchard too, understood by anthropology; it would give a record based on the closest empirical work for other sciences to use. Thus, despite his critique of the fallacy of functionalism as an exclusive method, his vision of anthropology scarcely differs from that of Malinowski. And about Malinowski, no words seem to me better than Jarvie's recent incisive critique:

. . . Malinowski by his relativism changed the whole metaphysical background to social anthropology. The basic problem was "how do we explain man's differences?" The Greeks said because they are fundamental, the rationalists said because they are superficial, the evolutionists said by development, the diffusionist said by the accidents of contact and borrowing. Malinowski (in my interpretation) says, "Bosh! There are no differences to be explained: there is only the miraculous diversity of mankind and his works. The problem of anthropology is now simply observing, describing and cataloguing this diversity."[44]

The burden of Jarvie's argument is that anthropology has fallen away from its once-great calling, that it needs to get back to grand theory and speculation, that it now seeks shelter in narrow methodology and circumscribed problems, simply because they are scientifically safe, on the model of the other sciences. Jarvie wants us to get back to big, even metaphysical, problems, to truly synthetic thinking. Others, too, like Derek Freeman, want a return to the really basic issues and hope that out of such a return a truly unified science of man will develop, which will link man's cultural, psychological, and historical natures, now hopelessly parceled out to the disciplines.[45] And this is the state of the problem at the present time.

With this brief sketch of the outcome of anthropology in the two major Anglo-Saxon countries we can draw this part of our essay to a close. We can also judge that the two major attempts to make

the science of man manageable both failed. The unilinear evolutionists were overambitious in their generalizations and did violence to the enormous range of facts that the new science was
bringing forth. The disciplinary alternative, while avoiding the
rash synthesis, actually succeeded in losing the necessary synthetic
vision. Gusdorf has aptly called the second alternative under-
ambition. There can be no doubt in anyone's mind that the under-
ambition of the discipline of anthropology has reaped, and
continues to reap, great and necessary empirical fruit. It is very
probable that there was historically no alternative to this necessary
development. But the point of my critique is that the science of
man, in losing the synthetic vision, actually lost the three things
that gave it such world-historical promise in the eyes of the eighteenth and nineteenth centuries. And if we are again going to make
the science of man meaningful in the way that Gusdorf and Jarvie
hope, we must find some kind of conceptual framework which will
permit us to reintegrate these three things into a single scientific
vision that includes 1) the central problem of the science of man:
How do we explain human differences? 2) the large historical
panorama of human development, which provides the background
and support for this explanation; 3) the superordinate value scale
for judging the wisdom and adequacy of man's social arrangements.

It is to this task that we now turn.

2   The Road Back to the Science of Man

If E. Adamson Hoebel is correct, Evans-Pritchard's two essays
on history and anthropology "should sound the close to a half-century era of anti-historicism in social anthropology."[46] The question

now before us is what kind of historical reorientation will enable us to rediscover the lost science of man? After our lingering review of the outcome of the discipline, represented by a few selected thinkers, the reader should be happy to learn that the solution to the complex and perplexed situation is remarkably simple. All we have to do is find an authentic line of historical inquiry that does not do violence to the multitude of special facts of the various disciplines. The question to decide is what will be our criterion for "authentic"?

The first thing we have to note is that Evans-Pritchard's was hardly the first major voice to lament the decline of history in the science of man. Almost a half-century ago both Harry Elmer Barnes and Alexander Goldenweiser had seen and understood the problem. It was not a simple matter of unilinear evolution *or* disciplinary specialization on ahistorical problems. Rather, there was a need for a third alternative, a genuine synthetic framework. Barnes's reflection is still contemporary:

> This collapse of historical sociology after 1900 was doubly disastrous, for it was during just this time that the critical anthropologists and the well-trained social historians [Green, Blok, Rambaud, Lamprecht, Breysig, Steinhausen, Turner, Shotwell, Beard, were building on better foundations than social Darwinism, or the earlier comparative anthropology uncritically in the service of unilinear evolutionism. But now there is no one, or very few, to take advantage, in historical sociology, of these new achieved results, and this careful work, which] will yield significant results of a permanently valuable character.[47]

And Goldenweiser, writing in the same journal, is also worth quoting at length, for his equally contemporary view:

> It must not be imagined that the critical school represents the last word in the advance of anthropological thought. [Far from

it: it is shy of synthesis, the courage to speculate, the generalizing imagination; it is timid with ideas, skeptical in the face of hypotheses.] Related to the last point is the relative neglect of the developmental aspect of culture. [The rejection of evolutionary theory does not mean that there is no development in civilization; it will be a more difficult problem,] but the task will not be denied. The universality, the regularity, the gradual character of the evolutionary process, may be rejected [but if one's aim is less pretentious evolution can still hold its own] . . . certain principles or trends of development may well be discerned . . . a different type of reconstruction of origins or early developments is coming to the fore. Such origins are not posited as specific historic happenings placed at the inception of an evolutionary series and fit to explain its nature. No, they are avowedly speculative constructs. . . . The trouble with the comparative method of the evolutionist lay in the uncritical acceptance of material and the utilization of static units to bolster up a dynamic conception. When buttressed with critical safeguards and applied to purposes which it is fit to serve, the comparative method emerges as one of the most valuable tools of historic and prehistoric research.[48]

This is still our problem: the reintegration of history for a truly courageous, speculative, and synthetic view of human evolution. It asks for considerably more than Evans-Pritchard. It is not the parceling out of anthropology to the other disciplines but rather a call to a truly mature science of man based on historical synthesis. The question that Goldenweiser so well leads up to is the one we suggested above: "What *purposes* is such a conception *fit* to serve?"

The Historical Purpose of the Science of Man

The science of man grew out of the crisis of the eighteenth century, and the nineteenth century inherited the crisis. It was a *moral* crisis. The medieval world view had loosened its hold on society, and now there was nothing to replace it. Whereas the Church had offered the one thing that man needs as much as the air he breathes—a dependable code of behavior for himself and his fellow man—it was precisely this that was now wanting. Society was headed for the kind of chaos that *Homo sapiens* fears most: the chaos of undependable and immoral behavior in his fellow men, the chaos of unregulated, irresponsible social life.

The science of man, let it be emphasized once and for all, had the solution of this moral crisis as its central and abiding purpose. Why build a science of man in society? In order to have a sound basis for a new moral creed, an agreed, factual body of knowledge that men of good will could use to lay down laws for a new social order. When we get a more or less reliable and reasonably rich knowledge of what man is and how things came to be as they are, we will have the basis for a new morality. Not a supernatural morality, like the defunct one of the Church, but a positive morality based on empirically demonstrated facts. This was Comte's vision, and his whole *raison-d'être,* and Comte was merely carrying out the mandate of the eighteenth century.

The valid historical synthesis that we are seeking would be one that *fulfilled this moral purpose.* No less. And we do not have far to look. All we have to do is to interrogate the nineteenth century in a way in which neither the unilinear evolutionists nor the critical discipline of anthropology did.

Let us go back to one of the fathers of modern anthropology, Theodore Waitz, to find the real purpose of anthropology. In his famous *Introduction to Anthropology,* which fell just about in the middle of the century, we find a familiar lament. And we should not be surprised at this point to be told that this lament is very contemporary; Waitz complained of the fragmentation of the disciplines and their mutual ignorance. It was all due, as we well know, to the scientific upsurge of that time, and it was also a reaction against the demise of the speculative philosophy of Hegel and Schelling. But it led to a compartmentalization in all fields, physical and mental.

The result was that the new scientific proliferation prevented the very task that it set itself, namely, understanding human nature. What was needed in Waitz's time was a new grasp of history based on empirical knowledge of all the disciplines. This is the original vision of anthropology, or the science of man, or the science of mankind—all three terms used interchangeably by Waitz (1863).[49] Furthermore, in an explanation quite unusual today, Waitz defined anthropology as embracing all peoples of the earth "including those who have no history . . . [Anthropology thus] endeavors partly to sketch an ante-historical picture. . . ."[50] In other words, anthropology did not embrace prehistory primarily; it was mostly a vision of the evolution of mankind *in history.*

But the meat of Waitz's book is the purpose for which it was written, which was not simply for evolutionary reconstruction in itself. Waitz set out to prove the irrelevance of species differences and the need for a conception of the psychic unity of mankind. The reason was to counter the facile propagandist version of Western superiority, which justifies the ongoing exploitation of man in society. In Waitz's words:

If there be various species of mankind [so goes the argument], there must be a natural aristocracy among them, a dominant white species as opposed to the lower races who by their origin are destined to serve the nobility of mankind, and may be tamed, trained, and used like domestic animals, or may, according to circumstances, be fattened or used for physiological or other experiments without any compunction. . . . All wars of extermination, when the lower species are in the way of the white man, are then . . . fully justifiable, since a physical existence only is destroyed. . . . [And Waitz concludes] To such or similar conclusions, the theory of specific differences among mankind leads us. Thus there are different and more comprehensive interests attached to the question of the unity of the human species, than to the probably unsolvable problem of descent from one pair or several pairs, or the contest about permanence or mutability of races.[51]

There is no question in this inspiring "research paradigm" about the moral thrust of the *Introduction to Anthropology*. Waitz's study is divided into two parts, both directed to the above problem. The first examined whether all human beings are of the same species on physical grounds, the second whether they are so or not on psychological grounds. And, of course, Waitz's findings in both cases were negative. If the people who held the idea of racial inferiority had been able to establish their case, they would have given a picture of evolution that would yield a sort of scientific "natural law" of the superiority of white Western civilization. If everything was there in the hard facts of physiology, then man could read nature for the new morality that he sought. Thus Waitz was to anthropology what Helvétius was earlier to Montesquieu's science of man. He wanted no physical determinism that would limit human freedom in creating a better world.

Like Waitz, Samuel Butler had a clear view of what was at stake, and I cannot resist quoting his delightful image:

. . . the principal varieties and sub-varieties of the human race
are not now to be looked for among the negroes, the Circassians,
the Malays, or the American aborigines, but among the rich and
the poor. The difference in physical organization between these
two species of man is far greater than that between the so-called
types of humanity. The rich man can go from here to England
whenever he feels so inclined. The legs of the other are by an
invisible fatality prevented from carrying him beyond certain
narrow limits. Neither rich nor poor as yet see the philosophy
of the thing, or admit that he who can tack a portion of one of
the P. & O. boats on to his identity is a much more highly or-
ganised being than one who cannot.[52]

Waitz and Butler were hardly alone in their focus on the moral
dilemmas of their time; these views were part of the great debate
of the nineteenth century on the problem of Negro equality, a
debate in which E. B. Tylor also had a central place.[53] But when
the unilinear evolutionists showed that all societies could po-
tentially evolve in the direction of civilization, they actually justified Western society as the pinnacle of achievement. Thus their
views could be a comfort to those intent on keeping the *status quo,*
or the new commercial-industrial economic system. This is how
Herbert Spencer's views were used. He provided a "scientific"
justification for the kind of world the financial investor held dear-
est to heart. And Frazer pronounced that world the most rational.

The Partial Achievement
of the Purpose of Anthropology, from Waitz to Boas

When unilinear evolutionism was overthrown, a large part of
the purpose of Waitz's anthropology was achieved. And this is
the most fascinating part of the whole development of scientific

anthropology up to Boas: it partly fulfilled its historical purpose. Boas was, as we saw, a pivotal figure, by which we mean that he kept at least part of the clear vision of the historical moral task of his science. By discrediting unilinear evolutionism, the superiority of Western society, and hence its right to exploit other races, was also scientifically discredited. Boas affirmed that what had appeared as racial differences was really a matter of historical differences, of environmental opportunity working diversely on a fundamentally similar basic human nature. He showed that everything depended on the size of the group, its contacts with outside groups, and so on. Even the fable of linguistic superiority vanished under his incisive thrusts. (The recent stand by the American Anthropological Association against racism was merely a restatement of what had long been conclusively achieved but had not become part of the laymen's world view.)

The general equality of the races was established on the psychic unity of mankind and its psychological equality, exactly as Waitz had wanted. Along with all this, cultural relativity was a logical complement, and here Boas put the crown on the whole development of self-scrutiny going back to Baron de Lahontan and the early eighteenth century. The need to study anthropology as a means of liberation from the constraints of one's own society, was, as we said, in the direct lineage of Rousseau's enjoinder. But now there was a conclusive, empirical background supporting this enjoinder: Western society could not adduce any facts to support its delusions of innate superiority.

From this development we must conclude that the discipline of anthropology, like the earlier science of man and the sister discipline of sociology was committed to the fulfillment of a moral purpose, and that there was a tradition of anthropology which stressed this moral purpose as its central aim. It was not simply a matter of choosing between the megalomania of unilinear evolutionism and the fetishism of disinterested, disciplinary science. Waitz carried on the Enlightenment mandate for a science of man that would usher in a new and better life based on a new and sounder system of social morality; Boas furthered it, too. Thus, when we consult Haddon's early *History of Anthropology,* we find that he places it in the lineage of Comte, Westermarck, and Hobhouse. And to be in the lineage of these men means to be involved directly in fulfilling the Enlightenment mandate.

What happened then? As Comte taught us, you cannot fulfill the enjoinder of providing a new system of morality, a positive morality, unless you have a unification of the various sciences into a single scheme. You have to be able to bring all your knowledge to bear on the social problem, and the only way you can do this is to present the knowledge in its cumulative, synthetic form. Otherwise, in science, as in life, all is disjointed, all is chaos; everything points in a thousand different directions. But as we saw earlier, this is just what happened to the science of man after Comte. It broke off into a number of pieces and so lost both its moral commitment and its necessary unified framework. The tragic *dénouement,* then, was that when Boasian anthropology actually achieved, at least in part, what Waitz and the Enlightenment had set out to do, this achievement was no longer recognized as the fullfillment of a central moral task.

Boas tried to keep the earlier vision alive by proposing that anthropology be used as a supplement to education. And when Redfield, too, tried to remain in this tradition, he had to appeal its central question as an afterthought: "What is the good life?" With both of these men the point of the spear had no force, because it lacked a driving shaft—a unified framework to carry the moral criticism. No wonder that anthropology failed to revitalize liberal education. It was no more than an historical-critical attitude that belonged to all the disciplines and to any man who wanted to use it.

Thus, like the defunct classics programs that anthropology should really have replaced and revitalized, anthropology failed in its turn. It gave no more than did the classics programs: a sobering, broadening, wordly attitude but not a deep-going, fundamental critique of the shibboleths of society. This kind of critique could have been given only by a science of man conscious of its historical task and its own unified power.* This means that the science of man would have had to include in one synthetic vision not only the achievement from Waitz through Boas, but also that of Marx, Veblen, and the whole tradition of critical sociology. It was just this kind of unification of the fragmented sciences that Waitz himself called for; it alone could give a picture of what happened in both history and prehistory, show how societies functioned on both small and large scales in all climates and in all types of material and social development.

When we lament this loss of a critical framework based on the moral mandate of the merged disciplines, we can understand why anthropology in someone like Lowie often assumed such a pathetically ineffectual nature. Lowie had forgotten what it was all about. Let us turn to his own words one last time for the eloquent testimony we seek. Was it a question of finding the causes of things, of why things happened as they did? Rest assured, Lowie tells us; he is familiar with the literature on the problem of causality in Hume and Kant and knows of Mach's and Russell's attempts to supplant causality with the mathematical notion of function. Then he says:

> . . . the distinction, however, seems unessential. The question is simply whether ethnology can give satisfactory reasons why cultural phenomena are as they are. To a certain extent the answer has already been given. Every ecological interpretation involves at least one definite determinant of the fact to be ac-

* See our discussion of the *idéologues* in the previous essay.

counted for. The Chaco tribes ceased to make stone tools in their present habitat because they no longer had the raw material; Australians do not grind stone when the diorite suitable for such a technique is beyond reach, etc.[54]

This is surely an imaginative outcome of Enlightenment science, of Waitz's labors. Perhaps even a narrow positivist, living through the present crisis in science and in the world at large, might feel some slight stir of discomfort over the range and nature of Lowie's interest in why we have come to be as we are, why our civilization is where it is today. The rest of us have only to ponder the inadequacy of these words in light of the problem of the science of man and hence to man himself. But I hasten to add that this is not a critique of Lowie. It is rather a demonstration of exactly why and how someone of Lowie's incisive analytic powers and broad interests could go astray and lose the earlier spirit of anthropology. The framework based on a primary moral enjoinder had disappeared, and thus one no longer knew what "why" questions to ask. The study of the processes of culture, mapped out by Boas as the principal task of the discipline, became an end in itself.

The question now was, Are we to study acculturation endlessly? Is there no aim or purpose for which to marshal our knowledge at any given historical period and bring it to bear on social questions? As Boas himself stated, all data become historical data as soon as they are collected. Everything is in flux in his Jamesian universe; hence, everything has to be called to account, or it is fated to become merely a dry record of historical fact. This would be useful, but only for a new kind of breed: the disinterested disciplinary scholar—a type that the men of the Enlightenment had not foreseen, and one they would be quick to renounce.

Was it possible that the science of man was conjured up to no human purpose? It was not only possible; in the first half of the twentieth century it was actual. These new men lived with an impossible fantasy; they were working for and gradually building and passing on to other new men who would gradually build and pass on a scientific picture of the human world. Of course, it was never complete. It could never be finished; therefore, they had to keep working on it, just because it was never complete and could never be finished. What use was an incomplete scientific picture? Not much use, they said. That's why we have to keep completing it. But, we retort, it will never be complete; you admit this yourself. Hence, it will never be of use. Well, they might finally answer, if we make it less incomplete, it might be less useless.

The Rediscovery of the
Authentic Tradition of the Science of Man

So much, then, for a science that lost its proper framework, that forgot it had grown out of the moral crisis of the eighteenth century. Even in its present state, the labor of the last hundred years has hardly been in vain; there should be no question about this. Anthropology had found out that the early nineteenth-century scientists were wrong to read racial differences for moral principles, also that the later nineteenth-century thinkers were wrong to read historical evolution for moral principles; it fully realized that the new moral principles had to come from empirical data. But, as we have seen, when it began to articulate these data it gradually lost the moral enjoinder. The fog had lifted, but it no longer knew where it wanted to go.

The exciting thing about our present vantage point is that we can see exactly what went wrong, and we can see the right road that was missed in this historical development. It is not that we are any brighter than these men; it is just that we do not have to repeat their mistakes. And we cannot allow ourselves to repeat them. Along with the resolution of their errors, history has served up the cost of those errors to us—the full historical crisis that we have to face. So let us now take this vital road that these great men had missed.

We have been able to see, in the development from Waitz to Boas, an authentic tradition for the science of man. We have seen that this tradition is one that stresses the synthesis of the disciplines in order to focus on the social moral problem. It would scan the whole range of societies in history and prehistory in order to answer the question of a new moral code. Now we are in a position to understand a great and crucial aspect of the failure of the Waitz-Boas tradition itself, namely, that it did not keep to the proper question for laying the basis of this moral code.

If it is an authentic historical tradition, it has to answer the central problem of the science of man, which we have repeated again and again: "How to explain human differences?" But in order to make this central problem a meaningful one morally the further question must be asked: "*What* human differences?" And what makes this question so difficult and crucial is that the answer to it must at the same time be a key to the basis for a new moral code. It could not be, as we saw, the difference in hair texture between races, as the early nineteenth century wanted; nor could it be the mere difference in the availability of diorite in one culture or another, as Lowie would have it. These differences are simply irrelevant to the problem of social morality.

What, then, is relevant, supremely relevant? Nothing else but the question: "What are the differences *in human freedom,* in societies, across the span of history?" It is only when we ask this question that we can see the moral usefulness of the science of man. It is only when we ask this question that we can see cultural relativity as the critique of all societies everywhere. And we can understand further that the idea of cultural relativity has failed precisely because it did not set up the standard of human freedom as the superordinate one. We know that the question of freedom, of maximum human liberation, was uppermost in Boas's mind and primary in Waitz's work. Their failure, then, is not a personal one; it really reflects the failure of all the disciplines to unite their science around this question as the central one for joint work. In other words, as we know so well by now, it was the failure of disciplinary science, the failure that Comte, Waitz, and others tried to remedy right at the start, but that continued to its ineluctable *dénouement* with the successors of Boas.

The Twofold Approach to the Problem of Freedom

We have been able to answer simply the question, "What is the larger theoretical critical framework to which we must turn to get back to the fundamental questions on which the science of man began?" It is the answer to Jarvie's entreaty, Gusdorf's critique, Freeman's hope—the answer to the whole contemporary failure of the various disciplines to be humanly relevant in our time, or in any time. When we ask what caused things to develop as they are now, how man in society got to be as he is, the only relevant principle must be the principle of human freedom; the only possible synthetic framework must be one that explains differences in human freedom in society and history.

A   The Origins of Inequality

Whenever we turn to a truly significant question—one that illuminates for us a clear path through the maze of scholarly accumulated work, through the subtleties of philosophical logic, through the vested interests and narrow visions of any group— we sense the great presence of Jean-Jacques Rousseau. It is truly amazing how he had conceptualized what is basic in our social-scientific dilemmas. Do we want to know how to read history for a moral enjoinder? Very simple, answers Rousseau. Read history as the saga of the origin and evolution of human inequalities. Read history as the development of the exploitation of man by man.

In his famous *Discourse on the Origins of Inequality* Rousseau postulated a primitive state of man, in which there existed no exploitation or unhappiness. The inequality began when one man laid claim to a piece of land and called it "mine," and the whole mad tourbillion of history began. Man is born pure and innocent, said Rousseau, but he is corrupted by what he learns in society. The primitive state, the state of nature, should thus be held up as an ideal to measure the whole gamut of vicissitudes that man undergoes in the artificial world of so-called civilized life.

We can have no true idea—unless we have given long thought and study to the problem—how world-shaking this simple speculation of Rousseau's was. It gave rise to endless speculations and an incredibly voluminous and long tradition of empirical work, which stretched through the whole nineteenth century up to the present day. It influenced Kant to make his own speculations about the origin of things; it influenced Marx in his reading of history as the history of economic exploitation; it influenced Proudhon when he pronounced, "Property is theft"; it influenced the Scottish philosophers to study and speculate on the problem; it actually determines the nature of Russian anthropology today. And, finally, it may help us to reorient ourselves, at least in part, to the proper framework of synthesis for the science of man.

Let us try to hit some of the high points in this extremely rich and complex tradition and so make some sense out of it. Naturally,

I must limit myself to a very small part of all the work that this tradition encompasses, partly to keep my essay manageable, and partly through sheer ignorance and helplessness in the face of it. It literally crams our library stacks and would take a lifetime to go through.

One of the thorniest and continuing debates on Rousseau's speculation on the state of nature has been over just what he meant by it, how seriously he took it. The debate stretches from the time of Lord Monboddo, through Ernst Cassirer, and into contemporary anthropology.* Monboddo in 1784 had a correct understanding, which must today still be ours, that Rousseau meant the "state of nature" to be an ideal model of the elemental condition of man. In Monboddo's words, which echo those of Rousseau in the "Preface" to the *Origins of Inequality:* "If such a state did never actually exist, which many believe to be the case, it would not be improper to use it as an hypothesis, in order to show what Man, considered as a mere Animal, is."[55]

The eighteenth century began with a search for the primitive and used him as a standard to show up the corruptions of effete, civilized life. The debate raged in the *philosophes* around Rousseau, and he immortalized it by giving it literary and scientific form. He sent voyagers looking for the state of nature and for the original nature of man, which he had pronounced innocent. As we noted earlier, Kant agreed that such a voyage was properly called an "anthropological" one. Perhaps the most recent noted anthropologist to make such a voyage was Claude Lévi-Strauss, who went to the Amazon. But the major problem of which we are now speaking was the one of the precise origins of inequality, and this is the tableau that we promised to sketch in vague outline.

Monboddo, who mentions the *Discourse* of Rousseau,[56] was

* See *Current Anthropology*, Vol. 7, No. 2 (April 1966), 196 ff.

one of the first to take up the speculation, and he claimed to have proved that the state of nature actually existed and still exists in some tribes, and thus is more than an hypothesis. And it is interesting to note here that the fight for the integrity of the science of man vis-à-vis physics was already clearly conceptualized by him, since he took a passing jab at the "manual philosophers" (Newtonian materialists and strict experimentalists!), who will not believe any data that are not right under their noses.* Monboddo had—needless to say—enormous good sense, and we will return to the real burden of his anti-Newtonianism in the concluding section of our essay. But he was also very gullible, as were most men of his time, in his belief in travelers' accounts, and he swallowed the story of an orangutan that was used as a cabin boy aboard ship and that died of deflated self-esteem when it was harshly criticized by the ship's captain.

Along with Monboddo, Hume speculated on this problem, as did Adam Ferguson in his *History of Civil Society* (1782).[58] Ferguson presented a good discussion, using Roman history and ethnographic sources, of the origins of rank, property rights, primitive democracy, the rise of inequality and tyranny. He had evidently seen the American Indians firsthand.

John Millar, another Scottish philosopher, wrote an excellent book, *The Origin of the Distinction of Ranks* (1793), in which he saw that men who live in the hunting and fishing stage of culture "have no opportunity of acquiring any considerable prop-

---

* Even more interesting, perhaps, is that this jab had its historic echo in a complaint by the anthropologist Kroeber long after the laboratory experimental tradition had established its hegemony on the disciplines. Kroeber complained that "the golden opportunity of basing on the behavior of whole living animals in a state of nature, first by observation, then by controlled observation, and finally by experiment at critical points—this opportunity was largely overlooked . . . in favor of the magic fetish of laboratory experiment and test that had done wonders with inorganic material."[57]

erty; and there are no distinctions in the rank of individuals, but those which arise from their personal qualities, either of mind or body."[59] A very contemporary insight, as any anthropologist will realize, since it had to be reiterated by Boas and Lowie, as we will see below. Millar went on to state that among animal herders something new comes into being: a new source of authority based on differential wealth, which "is not only greater than that which arises from mere personal accomplishments, but also more stable and permanent."[60]

With the settling of a permanent territory, land and permanent authority come into being. Military expeditions tighten society further into steady, hierarchical authority structures, which are reinforced by the priestly arrogation of heavenly support.[61] The stage of feudalism comes into being as subject peoples are settled into a durable structure of legalized exploitation, and this feudalism is everywhere similar, in East and West. Lastly comes the rise of merchant classes, trade, the standing army, and also the rise of ideas of liberty, the "social mobility" of peasants turned traders, and so on.[62]

I give this sketch from Millar because it is the more or less standard one of the time and the model for later additions and modifications of detail in both fact and theory. Adam Smith, Herder, Wilhelm von Humboldt, and also Kant, as we said, speculated on this panorama. Kant's essay, "Conjectural Beginnings of Human History," was very Rousseauian: he agreed that civilization had fouled man's earlier equality. Later on, in the nineteenth century, a whole host of thinkers pored over the question (see J. M. Robertson).[63] Buckle put forth his theory about the rise of the great primary civilizations; Bachofen, McLennan, Lubbock, and Tylor speculated on the life of the primeval horde, Maine on early communities, Spencer on political institutions, Charles Letourneaux on the origin of property and the evolution of political structures.[64] The names are legion: Hugh Seebohm and Frederick Seebohm on Greek tribal society and the evolution of manorial structure; E. A. Freeman, F. Mueller-Lyer, and Kovalevski on social development, the development of the family; R. Petrucci on *Les Origines naturelles de la propriété*,[65] and the important work of Emile de Laveleye on *Primitive Property*.[66] One could go on and on if there was time and purpose to dig into these sources.

But we are hardly interested in mere cataloguing. The question we set out with was the search for a critical model by which to measure the differences in human freedom in society and history. And in order to get a grip on this problem we began with Rousseau's own answer in his idea of the origin of inequality through private ownership of land. We are interested in those writers whose work was aimed at this question and who wanted to study the origin of inequality for a moral purpose, namely, as a critique of the contemporary rule of private property over the lives of men and the oppressive effect and consequences of class differences. This is the vital tradition, and from it we must of course leave out the names of all the optimistic unilinear evolutionists, all the apologists for Western, *laissez-faire,* economic man. Thus we must stop and note that there are *two distinct currents* in the nineteenth-century search for the origins of civilized society:

1 The current stemming from Rousseau, which saw civilization as an evil based largely on economic exploitation and class differences established by coercion to maintain privilege.

2 The current stemming from Ferguson, Millar, Adam Smith, through Spencer, Tylor, and the rest, who understood how inequality got started but who concluded that it did not matter once it had begun, since its fruit—Western civilization—was worth all the evil that came out of it. Thus Ferguson said that primitive equality was fine, but man had to blur it out in order

to progress, and property is the progress. Kant belongs in this current too, since he reckoned that on the whole the evil of inequality is outbalanced by the good that resulted from it. Man had achieved too much to bemoan the price he had to pay. This was, in a sense, the precursor to Hegel's whole philosophy of history as the unfolding of human freedom.

I do not mean to imply that this second current comprised only rosy optimists and empty-headed apologists for property and its inequalities. This would be far from the truth. Adam Smith's vision called for reforms and deep-going economic measures— for example, the idea of a tax on land value that was later made famous by Henry George and his followers (see George,[67] and the urgent reminders of de Fremery).[68] The intent of this tax was precisely to do away with historical injustices in a gradual, legal, nonviolent way. Alas, it was already too radical and threatening to the mad-scrambling new society in the nineteenth century; today it would place Smith among the ultraleftists. Smith's heirs failed to carry through an intelligent program of political economy and instead put their trust in the institutions they already had, hoping these would magically assure the development of freedom through plenty.

Today we know that human freedom has not at all "unfolded," rather that what little there is risks "folding up" entirely. The radical element in Smith's vision has remained a museum piece, and it fell to people like Fourier, de Laveleye, Engels, Marx, Oppenheimer, and Veblen to insist that commercialism was not compatible with human freedom.

Veblen wrote a nice speculative sketch, "The Beginnings of Ownership,"[69] which drew on anthropological data to show that the capitalist idea of property was pure nonsense—that property was not the result of productive labor historically. It was just as Marx and others had argued. This tradition was wholly at odds with the apologists of commercial society. Whereas Maine had seen progress and civilization itself in the rise of landed property, de Laveleye saw "formidable dangers to society." He understood the real problem of the age, the fact that the rise of political equality had not solved the new nineteenth-century question of social equality and that this had to come with equal distribution of goods. He quoted Aristotle on this very question and concluded that the inequality of rich and poor had really led to the downfall of Greek and Roman civilization. It was the echo of Fourier: civilization was the battle of rich against poor. And in this kind of internecine fight the real enemy had been overlooked.

Who was the real enemy? The modern state. The task of these latter-day Rousseauians was to show on the basis of the soundest empirical data and theory how the state itself had arisen and functioned *as a structure of domination*. Whereas for Rousseau and those theorists who followed close upon him the origin of the state had been largely a misty, speculative, historical reconstruction, these nineteenth-century thinkers had to make it a sound, vital, scientific theory. Thus the burden of demonstration on this group was to show that in the primitive stage there was equalitarian communism—joint ownership of land and equal distribution of commodities—and that with the development of civilization private property and unequal distribution began, and that they began specifically through some kind of conquest or other coercive rule of man over his fellows.

What the Marxian tradition wanted to show was that the modern state itself grew out of these origins and that it was the exploitative vehicle of the propertied classes, that the whole structure of politics was built on the basis of economic inequalities and served to perpetuate them by dividing the spoils, and that these spoils were divided *legally* only because the laws were drawn up and based on the structure of exploitation embodied in the state. The masses had long since forgotten how all this got started, and they accepted the structure of laws as somehow "in the nature of things." The people now had to be reminded how things had been "in the beginning."

We can see, then, how the problem of the origin of the state became a crucial focus of the Rousseau-Marx tradition. When we understand it this way, we can also understand one of the basic hopes of Marxist millenarianism, namely, that in a truly free and humanistic society the state would wither away. The animus of the anarchists was of course the same. With the new great industrial productivity no longer harnessed to the legal structure of capitalist domination the new society would recapture the freedom and equalitarianism of primitive society, only on a higher level this time—as Lewis Henry Morgan had himself envisioned. For all these reasons we can see why Marx and Engels leaned so heavily on Morgan.

The anti-statists needed dependable empirical materials for their scientific socialism, and not merely the speculations of a Rousseau, a Ferguson, a Kames, or a Millar. This is where Morgan's epoch-making firsthand study of Iroquois kinship structures entered the picture. Morgan had provided the analysis of Indian kinship groups and how they functioned in an equalitarian manner, and this provided the very model of communal society before the rise of exploitation. This was just what the anti-statists wanted, since their empirical problem was to show precisely the development of the stage between the primitive and the despotic government of the primary civilizations. This was the stage that in Europe and Asia had taken place somewhere in the great darkness of prehistory.

After reading Morgan's writings, it was an easy task for the brilliant Engels to speculate that the Greek and Roman *gentes* must have been like the Iroquois blood groups. And so the mystery was cleared up. The earlier tribal brotherhood everywhere had developed into an exploitative state based on distinctions of property. The Iroquois Society provided, said Engels, nothing less than the main lines of the "prehistoric basis of our written history."[70] Engels had merely to fill in with his own researches on the German, Roman, and Celtic developments to get a similar picture of the origin of inequality in prehistory. Finally, Morgan's study was a special stimulus to Engels and Marx, because Morgan had used it as an empirical model of primitive brotherhood; he had based a whole panorama of social evolution on it, and this was just what the Rousseauian tradition had wanted from the very beginning.

In this way, a whole tradition of what came to be called "conflict sociology" developed, principally in the names of Ratzenhoffer, Gumplowicz, and Oppenheimer, which aimed at filling out the picture. Oppenheimer's important work, *The State*,[71] was a summing up of this tradition and at the same time an attempt to bring it definitively to bear as a standard of social criticism. Oppenheimer hoped that if it could be shown compellingly and conclusively how the state arose as a structure of domination, then man would have a mandate for changing the present state of capitalist economic inequality. He showed, as one example, how the state developed as a structure of domination through the exercise of power by animal herders over the sedentary agriculturists with whom they came into contact. At first, the relationship was one of robbery, plunder, and withdrawal on the part of the horse-mounted herders. Gradually, the horsemen allowed the goods of the agriculturists to stand and instead of destroying them began to exact regular tribute. Eventually, permanent centers of administrative control were founded, which also served to protect the tribute-paying farmer against other predatory invaders. All this gradually became fused into a unitary social ideology and system, justified by myth and divine sanction and embodied in a priestly class. Here we have a full-blown structure of institutionalized domination, the state.

I have given a sketch of Oppenheimer's theory of the origins of one type of state in conflict and conquest so that we can see how suggestive it is. At the same time we can observe that the picture is still too neat; it is a modern kin of Millar's early work. We would expect a veritable mountain of factual, empirical work that would contradict any neat, sequential theory of the state's origins. If we could show that Oppenheimer is correct, say, on the Hyksos empire in Egypt, we could adduce other examples to show that it did not happen that way. And this is exactly what we get—a long scientific argument unfolding up to the present day on exactly what happened. Let us examine just a few of the documents in this argument, since that will serve the purpose of our discussion, and since my own familiarity with the subject is very limited.

THE FAILURE OF THE ORIGINS OF INEQUALITY PARADIGM

Let me hasten to assure the reader that I do not intend to burden him with the details of this argument, an argument that in any case is familiar to the student of anthropology. What I am simply showing is that the tradition which tried to use the origin of inequality as a critical scientific model failed. And when we take in the whole sweep and breadth of the work that went into it, and the stature of the men who contributed to it, we can see that this failure was an historically momentous one. It meant nothing less than the abandonment of Rousseau's vision and the challenge laid down to the science of man.

The crash of the empirical-theoretical edifice that set out to prove scientifically the miscarriage of the economic development of society is a crash that still rumbles in the background of modern anthropology. So we must be very clear about exactly what happened and what was at stake. On the surface it may look as though it sufficed to argue back and forth on empirical aspects of the problem of the origin of the state. But this is only on the surface; it obscures what is at stake at a deeper level of the philosophy of social science. At this deeper level, the matter was already clear before the critical anthropological tradition of this century.

A major attack on the Rousseau tradition came from the noted scholar Fustel de Coulanges in the nineteenth century. In his book *The Origin of Property in Land* Fustel de Coulanges launched a type of learned attack that Lowie later made famous; he took on all those thinkers "who loved to picture to themselves mankind living together, when society was first formed, in a fraternal communism."[72] He took on von Maurer, P. Viollet, and de Laveleye, as well as the noted historians Lamprecht and Mommsen, and thus covered a half-century span of theory. He examined the documents that these theorists had based their case on—the studies of the Visigoths, the Alemani, Thuringians, Franks, Greeks, Romans—and showed how these scholars had picked out of the early records only what they wanted to find, and so, in effect, had misread them. Fustel de Coulanges concluded his scholarly study by saying that the evidence does not show that land has not ever been held in common; it does show that community in land has not yet been historically proved. "In short, an imposing structure has been erected out of a series of misunderstandings. National communism has been confused with the common ownership of the family; tenure in common has been confused with ownership in common; agrarian communism with village commons."[73]

What Fustel de Coulanges insisted on was a truly scientific use of historical facts. He says at the very end of his work that "never have 'original authorities' been so much lauded as to-day; never have they been used with so much levity."[74] And finally, as we might now expect, what kind of people are these thinkers, and who is their prototype mastermind? They are simply a class of minds that is taken by the idea learned from Rousseau.

By the time we get to the critical anthropology of this century, not only primitive communism but most of the other components of the origins of inequality paradigm are called into question. Did the state originate in war? Well, it was evident to many that on the primitive level there are often very peaceful mergers of clans and families. Thus Rudolf Holsti wrote an anticonflict theory on this basis.[75] W. C. MacLeod launched a stinging critique of the conflict theory in a Ph.D. dissertation (1924), in which he tried to show, using North American Indian materials, that in no empirical instance has a class formation of aristocracy been imposed by conquest on an unstratified group. Rather, said MacLeod, inequality arises naturally because of individual differences, and even some origins of feudalism can be explained in this way.[76] Lowie, on the other hand, was largely in agreement with Oppenheimer's thesis but said that it was a theory of the origin of caste, and not of the origin of the state, the problem of caste being merely a special case of the larger, more complex problem (1922).[77] As for the initial origins of inequality, Lowie finds these even on the primitive level, and he terms Morgan's thesis on primitive democracy a clear fallacy. Like MacLeod later, and Boas earlier, Lowie stresses the inequalities that arise in any social grouping, inequalities due to individual differences, and the opportunities and distinctions that these differences make possible.[78]

And so the argument of the experts has raged on up to people like Robert MacIver[79] and Lawrence Krader today.[80] It has been fairly well settled that the origin of the state out of a uniform primitive communism based on coercive methods simply cannot be proved. And it cannot be proved for two reasons. In the first place, "the reality is too complex," as Lowie and MacIver held in their criticism of Oppenheimer. Second as Fustel de Coulanges and MacLeod showed, what happened in prehistory cannot be historically documented. And so the origins of inequality paradigm, which Marx, Engels, Oppenheimer, and the whole Rousseau tradition tried to convert into a truly scientific problem, simply failed to carry any scientific weight. "Not convincing" was the expert judgment.

THE DÉNOUEMENT OF THE SCIENTIFIC PROBLEM

But alas for those who find Rousseau antipathetic. He is not to be disposed of so easily, as the never-ending volumes on him and his work that stuff our library stacks so eloquently attest. As we are learning today from the new and tougher historians of science, a scientific problem has never been historically merely a scientific problem. As T. S. Kuhn so well instructed us in his recent work, *The Structure of Scientific Revolutions,* a scientific theory is accepted as a scientific theory only because the community of scientists agree to accept it and work under it. If they turn away from it, or against it, even a good theory can suffer long oblivion and continued dispute, and a bad one be accepted with alacrity and smugness. Witness, for example, the treatment accorded to the work of C. Wright Mills by the sociological establishment during his lifetime.

There is something deeper at stake in the origins of inequality paradigm than merely its failure to marshal sufficient empirical weight. To make a complex matter simple, what is at stake is whether the community of social scientists want a moral-critical theory of their own social system, or whether they want an apologia for that system, which allows them to continue blithely with their narrow, disciplinary empirical work. Stated this baldly, my position may appear perverse, but the quandary is there for all to see. The Rousseau tradition failed because only a very few really wanted it, and they could not persuade their fellows, just as C. Wright Mills failed to persuade them. The clue to this failure could already be found in some of the people we mentioned earlier —Ferguson, Kant, Smith, Millar, and later the *laissez-faire* evolutionists. Primitive man might have had a more equalitarian life, they said, but when we tally up all we have gained over what was lost, we are really better off. The matter is already clear in the introduction to de Laveleye's Rousseauian work, an introduction written for the English edition by T. E. Cliffe Leslie. He says:

> Modern communism finds no precedent in the institutions of early society, its conceptions and aims are those of purely modern origin; and it neither can justify them on the ground of conformity with original sentiments of justice, nor, on the other hand, can be charged with going back to barbarism for its theory of rights. The original ownership of movables by communities shows that the early usages of mankind are not models for our imitation. . . . The truth is that the early forms of property were natural only in the sense of being the natural productions of an early state of the human mind. The forms natural in the present state of society are those in conformity with the development of human reason and with modern civilization.[81]

Cliffe Leslie, in a word, belongs to the non-Rousseauian tradition; he rejects a critical model that would pass judgment on the obviously superior state of the Western parliamentary world.

Thus we can see what is truly at stake here. By the time we get to someone like MacLeod and his 1931 book, *The Origin and History of Politics*, it is painfully obvious where the professor stands. The origin of the state can be explained without the intervention of "conquests, magic, or necessary economic organizational influences."[82] How can they better be explained? By the "psychophysical character of the leadership type of animal [a character which is] not acquired, but inherited. Families of leaders tended to produce leaders continuously."[83] MacLeod's basis for rejecting the conflict theory was that it happened too far back in history to be proved; his hypothesis also cannot be proved for the same reason, but, says he, it is rendered inherently probable because of the improbability of the alternate theories![84]

When we are treated to such grotesque exercises in logic, we know that something deeper is at stake, whether we find these exercises in a "scientific" textbook or in a political speech on Vietnam as the war to end all guerrilla wars. And the deeper dilemma, as we said above, is whether or not we wish to opt for a scientific theory that is critical of present social arrangements. This is the whole lesson of Rousseau's tradition and of Rousseau himself. If we have a stake in deep-going social change based on a critical model of present social arrangements, then MacIver's stricture on Oppenheimer, which held that his theory is not complete and too simple, will not carry weight. If we want to use social science to help us to understand what is killing us, what is causing us to fail to adapt to the new challenges of our historical period— then we will accept and be willing to work under even a sketchy theory as long as it gives us a suggestive picture of our plight. This is again part of the lesson of the Rousseau-Marx tradition. If we do not want this, then we can consider that the noted economist E. R. A. Seligman disposed once and for all of Marx's economic interpretation of history and bested Scott Nearing in 1922 in the famous argument over whether capitalism is or is not best for the United States. The critical-historical matter would then be settled once and for all.

The Rousseau tradition, of course, was partly at fault. It failed to heed Hume's great caution that you cannot read nature (or history) for moral precepts on which automatically to base your conduct. Marx, Engels, Oppenheimer, and their school erred in thinking that it was enough to build a convincing historical argument and that men of good will would thereby be moved to change the existing social structure. But we saw that they were not moved. You cannot read history for support of social ideals in any conclusive way. You can only find clues to what you think is desirable. If we stay on the level of the ideal, we can find cases to support it; if we try to make it a general empirical law, then we always find cases that are exceptions, and the law is thereby discredited. A reading of history, as the symbolic pragmatists have conclusively taught us, is always the gathering of facts under a point of view.*

The fallacy of "originism," the nineteenth-century search for precise origins of all and any aspects of human development and social life, was not so much that the origins are veiled in pre-history and thus can never be found. The fallacy was that even if they could be found they are only tangential to the main thrust of symbolic-critical history. As we saw from Cliffe Leslie, if we do not accept a certain moral and critical stance toward present conditions, then no amount of theory or fact on the origin of things can sway us. The whole lesson of the Rousseau tradition is that it was an ideology for the liberation of man from the mal-functional institutions of society, and this ideology is something that you opt for. The moral disquiet that the individual may feel in any particular epoch is not in the "nature" of the epoch; it is in his own emotions and dispositions, as Hume taught us. For Metternich war was moral progress. How can you argue sci-entifically against this? The challenge that Rousseau flung at the science of man was, in sum, the enjoinder to opt for a better world and to accept whatever clues to betterment it could find. But his tradition failed to deal sufficiently with the armor that society provides to cover the sensitivities of lesser men. And the masses as well as the leaders of the twentieth century, in politics as well as, alas, in science, are for the most part such lesser men.

* See F. J. E. Woodbridge's excellent summary of this whole problem, *The Purpose of History* (New York, 1916).

It is only in the light of the failure of this part of Rousseau's tradition and the reasons for that failure that we can get a bearing on our present situation. We have an excellent accumulation of empirical and theoretical materials, but we no longer know what to do with it; we have no basis of organization. Forty years ago the noted sociologist-historian Harry Elmer Barnes could still find it scientifically meaningful to review the problem of the origin of the State, the original nature of man, etc.[85] Today this kind of scientific interest seems irrelevant to most of the ongoing research. The discrediting of unilinear evolutionism had the same effect on the science of man that the earlier discrediting of Hegel had in the nineteenth century—as Waitz lamented. Science flourished, but the broad, synthetic views, which alone make scientific work humanly meaningful, were absent. By the time Lowie had finished his lifelong demolition of Lewis Henry Morgan (a demolition that resounded in all the graduate schools where teachers of anthropology were prepared and still echoes to the present day) no theory of general, unilinear evolution was acceptable. As a result, there was no place to fit works like P. N. Ure's *The Origin of Tyranny*,[86] an excellent study of the rise of tyranny in Athens attendant upon the development of coinage, or of Gunnar Landtman's lifelong work on the origins of inequality,[87] a work that represents the fullest summing up of the whole tradition stemming from Rousseau. And what of Benjamin Nelson's scholarly work in this same tradition—*The Idea of Usury: From Tribal Brotherhood to Universal Otherhood?*[88] How are we going to include and to make felt the relevant work of two such diverse writers as W. I. Thomas and A. M. Hocart on social origins?

By the time of World War II, this whole lineage had been dissipated, since it had nowhere to go. Where there was some attempt to keep a historical-synthetic view, as in France, it lacked the essential element of a valid synthesis. Henri Berr, for example, and the scholars that he grouped, tried to give a coherent picture of the origins and the development of civilization; the group continues to this day to refine its speculative and empirical work.* But as William F. Albright tersely summed up this effort so far: "Instead of synthesis Berr and his colleagues have produced part of an historical encyclopedia, characterized by many of the faults of a standard publisher's undertaking and by few of its virtues."[89]

Generally speaking, what is meant these days by "synthesis" is encyclopedic hodgepodge, conveniently placed between a limited number of covers and inconveniently priced for the scholar. The simple fact has to be repeated again and again, because most social scientists seem to ignore it: a synthesis means an organization of disparate data that is intimately linked together by being fused with a single, organizing principle. What is lacking in the Berr vision is precisely the synthetic principle that would give unity and immediate relevant weight to the historical panorama of human development. As we know so well by now, this principle has to be a moral one, since the science of man itself is in its own origin and nature a moral problem. And the moral organizing principle for the whole tradition of historical synthesis has to be the one set down by Rousseau: we must study historical inequality in the processes of its evolution in order to attack the problem of human freedom in our time. Nothing else will do to organize and make humanly relevant the welter of accumulated facts on man in nature and history.

The contemporary tragedy in the science of man is that there

---

* See, e.g., A. Moret's and G. Davy's *From Tribe to Empire* (New York, 1926), for their view of the development of totemic societies into potlatch societies, and hence into a feudalism of chiefs. And see the whole list of publications in the *Semaine de Synthèse* series.

is no longer any community of scientists that would accept a social-critical theoretical model for its science. The moral burden of early anthropology has been forgotten, and the arguments that now rage are only about fact, value-free fact. The new stirring in anthropology, largely under the impetus of Leslie White and his school, Julian Steward, and others, is attempting to make evolution again respectable, as Barnes and Goldenweiser had wanted, by showing it in all its multilinear diversity and complexity. But this historical reconstruction risks becoming the coldest and most detached of tasks, as if we anthropologists who did it were of another species or from another planet. It is as though it were not our story!

THE VIGOR AND THE INADEQUACY OF RUSSIAN MARXIST ANTHROPOLOGY

In the light of all this it will be no surprise to learn that those traditions that have kept alive the Rousseauian quest will also be those that are most vigorous. They are vigorous in an empirical way, because they are able to organize a vast manifold of data around a simple principle, such as the problem of freedom in history. And they are vigorous in an ethical way, since they use such a synthesis as a critique of present social conditions. This explains what to many of us has seemed a wrong-headed and anachronous insistence by Soviet anthropologists on the relevance of Morgan, long after our own critical anthropological tradition had "disposed" of him. The whole story is contained in one paragraph by a Russian anthropologist, Iu. I. Semenov:

> The entire course of development of ethnography, anthropology, and archaeology, while compelling the re-examination of various individual specific conclusions arrived at by Morgan and Engels, confirms the correctness of their basic and fundamental hypotheses at every step and to an ever-increasing degree. Ex-

perience demonstrates that only if we guide ourselves by these postulates is it possible to make sense of the vast amount of material being made available by research and to create a picture of primitive society that will increasingly correspond to reality. Objective truth is attainable only along the road pioneered by Morgan and Engels. Every other path leads away from the establishment of an integrated and valid theory of primitive society.[90]

In other words, Soviet anthropology has kept the unifying focus of the Enlightenment as it was embodied in the work of Morgan, Marx, Engels, Oppenheimer, and the others we have mentioned. Before we pass judgment on the adequacy of the Soviet vision, let us remind ourselves one final time what is at stake here.

The Enlightenment wanted a universal history of the development of mankind, and they wanted it for a purpose—the moral purpose of freedom in community. It was the vision of Lessing, Herder, Condorcet, Kant, and all their heirs. Perhaps the best and earliest phrasing of just what the problem was, was that by the great Immanuel Kant: it would be the task of future generations to gather together all the vast accumulation of careful empirical historical studies in order to solve the burning problem left by the decline of medieval society, namely, how to have maximum free individuality and maximum community, at the same time. This was the paradigm historical problem, which anthropology would provide the best data to solve. It was uppermost in the minds of some of the best thinkers of the nineteenth century in all fields—the great Russian sociologist Peter Lavrov, the German philosopher Hermann Lotze, the American Josiah Royce.

For Marx and Engels the problem of freedom and the meaning of history could be boiled down to primarily one of property relations and the class struggles waged around it. And this is what Soviet anthropology has inherited. Thus primitive society is still the model problem, because it is the model of classlessness and collective ownership of the means of production. The evil, as we saw, entered history in the form of the state; for Western man the paradigm of this problem is the formation of the Athenian state, so brilliantly glimpsed in its essentials by Engels.

This, finally, gave us that striking critical model of the nineteenth century, the model of the anti-statists, that of society versus the state. It was passed on all the way from Fourier to Oppenheimer, as we saw. And it was clearly conceptualized. It was the problem of the political structure of the division of the spoils versus the economic structure of the production of wealth. The vision was that historically the economic society would gradually replace the political structure through the emergence of machine-made plenty; the new machine-slaves would minister to the development of truly free citizens. We see an echo of this dichotomy in Veblen's idea of industry versus business. Remember, too, that Marx, following Hegel, said that history had to shatter the equanimity of the primitive paradise in order that the productive forces develop, and this would eventually lead man to true freedom. This was also Morgan's view, as we noted earlier.

The trouble is that the nineteenth century did not solve this ambiguous problem—not the anarchists, the Marxists, the Adam Smithians, the Comteans, the Proudhonians—no one. Everyone longed for the ideal community, and many looked back with wistfulness to both the primitive and the medieval times, when lust for power and gain was subordinate to moral social life, or, as Comte put it in his famous yearning, when politics was subordinated to morals. But it was only the Marxists who prided themselves on being realistic and scientific about the matter and who could thus actually predict the "withering away of the state."

I have dwelt upon this interlude in the history of passionate human visions only to highlight the inadequacy of Soviet anthropology. The problem of the state (versus society) that Marxism failed to solve has been inherited by the most statist of states. And this state loudly proclaims that its social scientists are solving the problem. It is a cynical turn of history and theory. American sociology dissipated the moral problem inherent in the society-versus-the-state paradigm by turning it into a strictly empirical one. Soviet social science has dissipated the moral problem by limiting it strictly to its economic, productive dimensions. In a word, it has forgotten what Marx and Engels had uppermost in mind—the problem of freedom in a true non-statist community.

Perhaps no one has better explained this paradoxical outcome of the Marxist vision into a full-blown oppressive statism than Martin Buber in his important work *Paths in Utopia*. Instead of going in a communal direction, to assure human freedom, Marxism went in a statist direction (see also Penty).[91] The whole problem of Marxism—and of Soviet social science—is summed up in this paradox. The rigid economic Marxists and the contemporary Russians have forgotten what was at stake in the theoretical problem of freedom. It was not merely a matter of the economic origins of inequality but something much more broad and complex. What was needed as a synthetic philosophy of history was nothing less than a complete theory of human alienation in society and history. To judge by a recent review of the *Festschrift* to C. Wright Mills, *The New Sociology*, Soviet social scientists recognize only the limited economic dimension of alienation.[92] And this is precisely where Marxism in its still unfinished form is not adequate as an organizing synthesis on the problem of human freedom.

Thus, in sum, the Soviet scientists have properly accused the West of dissipating the original vision and promise of the science of man; but in turn they are guilty of limiting this vision to only one of its aspects. As a result—need it be said?—their social scientists find themselves as much in servitude to the state and to its uncriticized social arrangement as do ours. In order to break through this impasse we will have to again remind ourselves of the contemporary relevence of the vision of Rousseau and turn to him in order to find the basis for a full examination of the problem of human freedom. As we said in the very beginning of this section of our essay, the problem of freedom has a twofold aspect. We have covered the first one, the origins of inequality, and we have been able to judge its explanatory power, its great historical importance, as well as its inadequacy. Let us now turn to the second aspect.

B   The Primitive Ideal Model
as a Critique of the Present Time

The origins of inequality paradigms fail, then, because they are not enough of a critical measure to illuminate the constrictions on human freedom in society today. They only show us what happened, or rather speculate on what happened, in some distant time. And what we need to know in order to have a fully vigorous moral imperative for the present time is what is "killing us" now. We need a secular moral code that answers to the problem of evil in society, just as the Middle Ages, whose problem we inherited, had their theocentric code. The model that we would use to measure the shortcomings of present social institutions would have to be an ideal image of man. It would have to be an image based solidly on what we know about human nature, on empirical fact; yet it would have to be a constructed model, going beyond man as he is to man as we wish him to be. This would give us something to aim at, something always to be attained; yet because it would be based on known facts about human nature, it would be more persuasive than a mere fantasy. We would hold up to man an image of the most developed person, the highest individuality, and at the same time the other image that keeps the tension of the paradox: an image of the most communal, equalitarian society. Thus it would serve both as a critique of the present and as a utopian figure to draw our best efforts.

This is the composite vision that Rousseau had in mind when he spoke of the "ideal" of the "primitive." The use to which he wanted it put was the utopian, social-critical use. There has been much dispute about what Rousseau meant in these "state-of-nature" speculations, as we noted earlier. But, as we said, the matter is quite clear. He used the ideal type in the same way that Plato had done in *The Republic*. The confusion is not Rousseau's but belongs to those who lost the Enlightenment vision of what was generally known as "ideal-real" science. This in itself is a great and neglected chapter in the history of ideas, this loss of the ideal-real dialectic in social science in the twentieth century. Its meaning was very clear, for example, to men like Bastian in anthropology, Brett in psychology, Lotze in philosophy, J. L. Myres in political science. They understood the ideal type in a way that later came to be narrowed down, as is best seen in its usage by Max Weber.[93]

For Weber, the ideal model was a fictional accentuation of empirical reality, created for the purpose of being able to gain some kind of conceptual grip on that reality. It was a way of including many disparate kinds of data into one sharp imaginative mold—whether or not this imaginative construction was exactly true. For the ideal-real science of Enlightenment, on the other hand, the ideal model served a moral-critical purpose as well as a scientific-conceptual one. It not only united disparate data, but also served to answer such pressing moral dilemmas as: What is the highest developed individuality? The "good life"?

For example, in the days when political science still partook of the Enlightenment quest, it was an ideal-real science that sought to answer one basic and central question, the question posed right at the beginning of modern political science by Aristotle: "What are the forces, as far as we know them now, that maintain or destroy states?" The "real" aspect of this question is the empirical data gathered on the actual forces that are destroying a given state. But these data cannot be given meaning unless they are played off against an "ideal" aspect, namely, what social forms would be necessary in order to make a new and intelligent adaptation to present historical conditions?

The important point that I wish to make is that without the "ideal" or critical aspect of social science, the "real" aspect is dissipated into an endless search for data, an infinite multiplication of special, technical problems; there is nothing to bring them into focus. J. L. Myres, who early in this century reminded us of Aristotle's question as the basis for political science, went on to bemoan the complexity of the problem: "But if a young student of political science were to set himself to this life work, where could he turn for his facts? What proportion of the knowable things about human societies . . . could he possibly bring into his survey, without a lifetime of personal research in every quarter of our planet?"[94]

The only answer to this is that he must look for the facts that reveal most directly the possible failure of his own political system to meet present world conditions. He must, as we said earlier, try to find those facts that explain why *he* is in danger of "being killed." Political science would then answer the question of the destruction of states anew in each historical epoch, so that citizens might take preventive action. This is why political science, if it is truly functional and dynamic, is inseparable from critical sociology.

It is no surprise that modern political science, having forsaken the Enlightenment tradition, is no longer able to answer Aristotle's question in a truly scientific way. In order to answer it political science would have to abandon its posture as a narrowly empirical discipline, "realistically" studying political behavior and instead join with a critical sociology that offers an ideal-real conception of the total social system. It is an interesting speculation, and I think an accurate one, to say that the best contemporary political science has tried to keep its vitality in a way that exempts it from coming to grips with its Enlightenment mandate by "including" the Enlightenment quest within a more "sophisticated" and superordinate vision.

I am thinking here of political theorists like Hans Morgenthau and his "realistic" political science, derived from Reinhold Niebuhr's vision of man. And Niebuhr, as we well know, aimed particularly to show in his life work the failure of the Enlightenment in modern thought. Thus, what these people are saying in effect is that states will be states because man will be man, and power is power, and corruption is eternal in the realm of finitude. In order to be realistic the political theorist must align himself with certain of the power thrusts of his national state, since this is the only way to "realistically" promote its more basic humanistic values against the totalitarianism and the untempered power of other states. The Nazi epoch is held to be the paradigm for this mature consciousness. Today, we can in our turn judge this new Greek-Christian "realism"; its bankruptcy is nowhere more apparent than in Morgenthau's support of the Diem regime in South Vietnam. It is a bankruptcy that Niebuhr himself now seems to realize in his latest writing; but if he was a "prophetic voice in our time" in the 1930's, as Tillich and others claimed, it is very clear that his time is past and he is no longer speaking intelligibly to the present world crisis.

This failure results, as we had every right to expect, specifically from the overdose of "realism" that slighted the necessary ideal-critical stance of the Enlightenment. These gentlemen spoke as though ideals had no prominent place in political science. The fitting comeuppance was given to Morgenthau by MacGeorge Bundy on the televised national teach-in over Vietnam in the spring of 1965. What right, said Bundy, had Morgenthau to imagine himself any better expert on Vietnam than anyone else, since he had already made the erroneous prediction on backing the Diem regime. Morgenthau was nonplused; he was a realist being realistically judged. In other words, by allying himself with the Government's "realistic" policy Morgenthau had forfeited the only vantage point that the social scientist might have: the ideal-critical stance, the higher moral judgment.

From all this it should again be very clear that the social scientists's primary attitude is one of social self-criticism. If he abandons it in time of national danger, he must be very sure about the present reality and the precise character of that danger. But if people of the stature of Niebuhr and Morgenthau go astray, perhaps there is no worthwhile caution that can be laid down, except to the young, that they not repeat the mistakes of their elders. Each historical period has its own mandate, and the task of youth is to find out exactly what it is, on its own terms. C. Wright Mills's work is a perfect ideal-real blend of political science and sociology. It gave a coherent picture of the functioning of the American social system with a view to forestalling the destruction of that system in World War III. Alas, the best testimonial to the failure of ideal-real science in the twentieth century is the fact that the social scientists turned their backs on Mills, and now the laboratory of international political events is relentlessly grinding out empirical support for Mills's ideal-real vision.

When we realize that it is precisely the loss of the ideal-real dialectic that characterizes contemporary social science, we can also get an insight into many of our disputes. For example, the continuing problem of the "primitive" that we noted earlier. Is the matter merely relative, and the primitive no different from modern man? Is modern man just as irrational, or even more so? Is primitive society more or less desirable than modern society? This is a debate that has quietly smoldered since the eighteenth century, as we noted earlier—from the Baron de Lahontan, through Rousseau and the *philosophes,* Fourier and the nineteenth century, up to modern anthropology today (cf. *Current Anthropology,* April 1966, and *The Concept of the Primitive*).[95]

It is clear that it is a sterile debate in its usual form. It is obvious, as it was to many in the eighteenth century, that primitive society and primitive man are in some ways superior to modern society and modern man, and in some ways distinctly inferior. The whole matter could be dismissed as relative, which it usually is. But then, look what we miss, what we throw out, namely, the whole collection of data on primitive societies since scientific anthropology began. We have gathered it for a purpose—a moral-critical purpose, as we know so well by now. What we must do in order to make this debate meaningful is to frame it in the terms Rousseau set up, that is, by integrating our knowledge of the primitive into an ideal-critical model of man. In this way, we have a basis for ideal-real science.

Whatever we find in primitive society that stands in judgment of our present conditions becomes a part of our model; whatever we see in communal society that serves as a clue to our deteriorated social arrangements goes into the construction of our model. Since we know that in many ways we have made definite and momentous gains over primitive and traditional society, we cannot limit ourselves to this one model. We need to construct an ideal-real image of man out of all the social-historical materials available to us. In this way, the whole panorama of evolution would make its weight felt. What does it tell us about what is wrong in our present conditions?

The task of social science in all the disciplines today is to proceed to the construction of such an ideal-real science. We must realize that none of our data makes full sense unless it is focused on present problems of human value, and if it is so focused, then even conjectural data become of vital importance. Take, as an example, a recent revival of evolutionary speculation in the writing of Robert N. Bellah. Bellah has offered a scheme of religious evolution that is at least partly speculative in nature. And as Pitirim Sorokin has recently said, it is not only speculative, but empirically false in part.[96] Bellah makes too much use of contemporary primitive societies (in this case the Australian aborigine) in explaining social origins and evolution. Anthropologists have long known that this is improper, that present primitive societies are the result of long developments—"historical" developments, but without any historical records (cf., e.g., Talcott Williams).[97]

Thus Bellah, repeating Durkheim's error, offers a scheme that is at least partly a fabrication, as Sorokin clearly sees. But we must remind ourselves here that Bellah is employing this scheme in a Weberian "ideal" sense to get a conceptualization of evolution by putting it into accentuated sequences, and he wants this scheme for Weberian purposes of objective analysis. So we can see where the trouble lies. It lies in limiting a speculative analysis to ostensible "value-free" purposes of functional analysis. Bellah is correct to revive speculative historical reconstructions, else how can we get a grip on the manifold of fact? Yet he is wrong to imagine that such reconstructions can ever be entirely empirically defensible, especially when they reach back into prehistory, as we learned from the origins of inequality debate.

If we are to use them at all, we must take a step forward into a new (rather, old) kind of science—away from Weber and back to the ideal-real usage of the nineteenth century. These speculations are justified only if they have present moral-critical relevance. Contemporary social scientists, like Rousseau's contemporaries,

Helvétius and Voltaire, have failed to understand the depth and vitality of the kind of science he proposed. Until they do, even the most earnest researchers will show themselves occasionally to be naïve and ill-informed and the most learned debaters will continue to talk past each other.

We must have an ideal-real science, then, and a full-field theory of alienation that rests on both aspects of the problem of freedom, as designed by Rousseau. We need the historical reconstruction, as well as the full-blown critique of present social structures. What would such a theory of alienation look like? It would largely be a "historical-social psychology," a picture of why man has failed to make the freest possible adaptations to new conditions in each historical period. It would take for granted that man could make such adaptations, that there is nothing in his nature that hinders his potential freedom. It would find the evil in social arrangements and in man's failure to act upon his social structure in a liberating way in any particular period.*

As a basis, then, we would accept—*must* accept—Rousseau's proposition that man is born pliable and neutral and is shaped by his society. In this way, we would bring Marxist thought in its full roundness up to date. We would not limit ourselves merely to the determinisms of economics—although they would play the largest part—but would also have to talk about a full theory of human nature in society, one, for example, that comprises the causes of mental illness, of crime and delinquency, of authoritarianism in religion and politics, of life styles and world views, of fanaticism and revivals, and so on.

In the light of this need for a truly broad and full theory of alienation it is important for us to study what is happening to so-

---

* Fortunately I need not repeat here the outline of such a theory of alienation since it is given in other writings. See, e.g., *Beyond Alienation* (New York, 1967) and *The Structure of Evil* (New York, 1968).

called Marxist theory in Russia today, as the Russians try to understand something like middle-class crime. In a recent study, for
example, it was found that the majority of juvenile delinquents in
Russia came not from the lower-income groups, but rather from
the middle-income group. How to explain this? Why would the
new and happy Soviet consumer stoop to crime? Had not Russia
solved the basic dimension of alienation—the private ownership
of the means of production? There can be no social-structural reason for this kind of crime, *ergo,* concludes this study, there is something in the mentality of these criminals that is responsible for their
behavior.[98] Here is a fitting ending indeed to the Marxian tradition.
If social arrangements are now so perfect that they cannot be accused, the blight must be in the individuals themselves! As we
shockingly learn in report after report, the dissidents in Russia
today are treated as mentally ill and are forcibly confined; how else
explain failures in paradise?

Fortunately, a study like this is counterbalanced by a recent excellent essay by A. Ia. Gurevich.[99] In it, the author is in effect calling
for a full-field theory of human alienation in society and history.
This is a reaching for the full flowering of the Enlightenment tradition of ideal-real science represented by the young Marx and somewhat slurred over by him in later years, then completely effaced
by most of his successors. This is something that social scientists
the world over must reach for and work toward, together if possible, across national boundaries. When all is said and done, we
have one common enemy, the target of our criticisms: the constric-
tive national state.

Probably the brilliant work of Erich Fromm is the best synthesis
of economic and psychological determinisms to emerge in our
epoch, and it is on this we shall have to build.

3   Conclusion: The Enormous Dimensions of the Problem

At the end of this sketch, let us hope that we have been able to argue effectively about one thing at least, that the science of man took root in the vision and moral dilemma of the eighteenth century, and that it was that century, largely in the person of Rousseau, which laid down the lines for the development of a valid Science of Man. I hope that I have also been able to show that this science has as its main task the maximization of both personal freedom and social community, the paradoxical and ambiguous challenge conceptualized by Kant. And, finally, I hope that it is plain that freedom as a *scientific* problem can only be conceptualized in its twofold aspect.

If we accept all this, we must now add that there is still another sense in which we must get back to the eighteenth century, and once we get back to it in this new spirit we shall discover still a third dimension of the problem of freedom. It is this aspect of the eighteenth century and this third dimension of the problem of freedom that show, perhaps best of all, how pitifully we have narrowed down and dissipated the grand promise of a science of man in society. Let us merely touch upon it now in closing this essay. It will help us draw together our critique of disciplinary fragmentation and specialization, and at the same time help us to see the real ground of our science in the realm of ethics. If we have inherited the problem of the decline of medieval society, then we must make clear that a science of man grounded in a new secular ethics is itself narrow and limited unless it can offer a total vision of reality. In other words, a full-field theory of alienation cannot have its fullest meaning if it is only two-dimensional. It must be not only historical and social but ontological.

Historians of science are now beginning to bring back into prominence something that has long been obscured: while we knew very well that the triumph of Newtonianism in all the sciences was what made the eighteenth century great, what was obscured by this triumph was precisely the countercurrent of a deep and anguished anti-Newtonianism.* It is only today that we can again see what was truly at stake in this struggle, simply because we are paying the full price of the sweeping victory of the one-sided Newtonian world view.

Several voices can be heard on this problem—voices in theology, like Reinhold Niebuhr's and Paul Tillich's, voices in the science of man, like Eric Voegelin's,[100] Alfred Weber's, and Albert Salomon's.[101] What they are calling for is a third dimension to the problem of freedom and human action, the dimension that has been slighted and almost forgotten in the great surge of objective, empirical science. It is the dimension of ontology that would once again give central prominence to the only questions capable of guiding life and science: What is the meaning of life? What is worth striving for? What may man hope for? Without these questions, as Voegelin has argued with such brilliance and massive scholarship, science itself is sickly and puerile at best. At worst, it is idiotic and actively antihuman.

We should not be surprised that one of the best minds and most colorful of men of the eighteenth century had already given the matter ample voice in his six volumes of *Antient Metaphysics*. Lord Monboddo's whole life was a protest against Newton and the new breed of "manual philosophers," what today we would call the new fetishists of science, the foreground manipulators, who

* See *Beyond Alienation* and *The Structure of Evil* for fuller details on this.

lost the depth and background of nature. Monboddo uttered a warning cry not to abandon the Greeks, not to lose the perspective of ontology in philosophy and science. He warned that we need to deepen the merely material approach to man and nature with the spiritual approach; and that we have as our central task the explaining of—and not simply describing—man's condition on earth.

Monboddo saw that beginning with Descartes and Newton a new type of man and attitude were becoming ascendant, and he was one of the few in the eighteenth century to realize that this new type of man was not necessarily for the good. He launched a massive attack on the new materialist causality that these men were championing, the secondary causality that took the burden of explanation. We now have to be content, warned Monboddo, with part explanation, with part philosophy, what Santayana later called in his criticism of Dewey, "philosophy of the foreground": manipulative, scientific, existential, experimental philosophy, which slights the background of nature, the "realm of essence" or substance. We need to keep in view, said Monboddo, the Aristotelian problem of final cause, and not merely material cause. We need to try and understand what life is all about, where it is heading. Otherwise, we ourselves will be headless, undirected, trivial men.

Alas for us, the protest represented by Monboddo lost out, and Newtonianism went on to a long victory substantiated by Darwin. It was he who fully legitimated the focus on material cause even in the life science, biology. But today, a century later, there is the new stirring that we noted above, which promises eventually to usher in an entirely new vision of science. Voegelin predicts that perhaps the most important single fact about the first half of this century will be the complete reappraisal of the character of the science of man. And I share this prediction, both in the sense in which Voegelin intends it—that the science of man will rediscover its grounding in metaphysics—and also in another sense, which has been only too much slighted: that the twentieth century will see the full crowning of the Enlightenment vision and will fashion a full-field theory of human alienation as the *empirical* basis of a unified science of society.

This means that we will have a model for the fullest liberation of man by making a complete accusation of social restraints on his freedom. It means that we will have a vision of a new community that would finally provide the fullest context for civilized living. But it means more as well. By reintroducing the dimension of ontology as the ultimate ground of human freedom, our model of man and community will not be a finished model, as the critics of a manipulative science so rightly fear. It will be only a beginning for the creation of a new man out of the still unknown and untapped energies of the life force itself.

In order for this to happen, the science of man, while working toward the new community, would be partly grounded in a creative new myth of the meaning of life. We would then have a science that would have gladdened the large heart of a Robert Redfield—a science of man with a vision of community, *working in a community that itself creates the new symbols of a new social order*. In other words, we would be scientists working within a living myth of the significance of our own science and of our own lives, scientists working with artists—in a sense subordinate to art because partaking of a creative mythology, as Comte's genius foresaw. In this way, and in this way alone, would our general theory of alienation have its fullest reach, since it would seek to overcome alienation not only in our "subjects," but also in ourselves, in the community of science. When we think of our present condition, which of us does not feel a wistful sigh at such a prospect? After all, the dream of truly free men is not only to annex the whole post-Socratic accumulation of knowledge; it is also to again rediscover something of the pre-Socratic mystery and awesomeness of the living world, to again feel a sense of intimacy with the cosmic process, to marvel at the rich miracle of creation. Scientists who would do this would not be narrow and manipulative rationalists, but, rather, like the "primitive" scientists that Wilhelm Reich longed for: festal, full, and warmly expansive, perhaps at last a type of anthropologist who would himself be a model for the primitives he studies.

Yes, this is all a dream, and perhaps that is the greatest lesson of the present crisis in science. We have learned that all our best knowledge is merely a symbolic counter for the dream of freedom. Perhaps one day we will have the ultimate courage, the courage to affirm a dream that mankind has collectively been spinning and mellowing for over 2,500 years. We would look in vain for more than a few men who have this kind of courage in the corridors of scientific power and prestige in our universities today. Yet, under the pressure of our world social crisis, the numbers are growing: man seems to reach for the conceptions needed to help him survive. The pressure of our present evolutionary crisis is directly upon man's brain. We can more confidently pass on the vision of the Enlightenment to our young today than perhaps at any other time since it was fashioned. The hope of the authentic spirit of ideal-real science, like that of the life that it was meant to serve, lies in the new birth that defies oblivion.

REFERENCES

1 The Tragic Paradox of
Albion Small and American Social Science

1 Thomas W. Goodspeed, "Albion W. Small," *American Journal of Sociology*, XXXII (1926), 12-13.
2 Edward C. Hayes, "Albion Small," in *American Masters of Social Science*, ed. Howard W. Odum (New York: Holt, 1927), pp. 149-150.
3 A. W. Small, *Adam Smith and Modern Sociology* (Chicago: University of Chicago Press, 1907), p. 22.
4 *Ibid.,* pp. 23-24.
5 *Ibid.,* pp. 65-66.
6 *Ibid.,* p. 238.
7 Hayes, p. 184.
8 A. W. Small, "The Methodology of the Social Problem," *American Journal of Sociology*, IV (1898-99), 114, 131.
9 A. W. Small, "Fifty years of Sociology in the U.S. (1865-1915)," reprinted in the *American Journal of Sociology Index, 1895-1947* (1915), 210.
10 *Ibid.,* p. 243.
11 Harry Elmer Barnes, "Albion W. Small and Modern Sociology," *American Journal of Sociology* (1926), 29.
12 A. W. Small, "The Future of Sociology," *Publications of the American Sociological Society*, XV (1920), 191-192.
13 A. W. Small, "Some Structural Material for the Idea 'Democracy'," *American Journal of Sociology*, XXV (1919-20), 258.
14 Small, "Fifty years of Sociology in the U.S.," p. 254.
15 A. W. Small, book review in *American Journal of Sociology*, XXXI (1925), 89.
16 A. W. Small, "Sociology," *Encyclopedia Americana* (1918), Vol. XXV.
17 *Ibid.*
18 Barnes, p. 39.
19 *Ibid.,* p. 19.
20 Small, "Fifty years of Sociology in the U.S.," p. 263.
21 *Ibid.,* p. 263.
22 Small, "The Future of Sociology," p. 192.
23 A. W. Small, "Some Researches into Research," *Journal of Applied Sociology*, IX (1924-25a), 101-102.

24 *Ibid.,* pp. 104-105.

25 Luther Bernard, *Origins of American Sociology* (New York: Crowell, 1943), p. 599.

26 A. W. Small, "Static and Dynamic Sociology," *American Journal of Sociology,* I (1895-96), 208.

27 A. W. Small, "The Significance of Sociology for Ethics," *The University of Chicago Decennial Publications,* 1st ser., Vol. 4 (Chicago, 1903), pp. 113-149.

28 Hayes, p. 156.

29 Bernard, p. 528.

30 Richard T. Ely, "The American Economic Association, 1885-1909, an Historical Sketch," *American Economic Association Quarterly,* 3rd series, Vol. 11 (1910).

31 A. W. Small, "The Future of Sociology," p. 188.

32 Barnes, p. 194.

33 Small, *The Meaning of Social Science,* pp. 236-237.

34 *Ibid.,* p. 243.

35 Small, *The Meaning of Social Science,* pp. 252-253.

36 *Ibid.,* pp. 269-271.

37 *Ibid.,* p. 254.

38 Joseph Schumpeter, *Economic Doctrine and Method, an Historical Sketch,* trans. R. Aris (London: Allen & Unwin, 1954), p. 154.

39 Gustav Cohn, *A History of Political Economy* (Philadelphia: American Academy of Political and Social Science, 1894), pp. 134-135.

40 A. W. Small and G. E. Vincent, *An Introduction to the Study of Society,* 1894 (Boston: American Book Company, 1894), chap. i.

41 A. W. Small, "Some Contributions to the History of Sociology," *American Journal of Sociology,* XXX (1924-25b), 302-303.

42 Small, "Sociology," p. 212.

43 A. W. Small, *General Sociology: An Exposition of the Main Development in Sociological Theory from Spencer to Ratzenhofer* (Chicago: University of Chicago Press, 1905), p. 40.

44 A. W. Small, unsigned article in *American Journal of Sociology,* XXVII (1921-22), 513.

45 Schumpeter, "Economic Doctrine and Method," p. 153*n.*

46 Alfred Weber, *Farewell to European History, or, The Conquest of Nihilism,* trans. R. F. C. Hull (New Haven: Yale University Press, 1948), pp. 146-147.

47 E. Becker, *The Structure of Evil: An Essay on the Unification of the Science of Man* (New York: George Braziller, 1968).

48 Small, *General Sociology,* p. 37.

49 Victor Branford, "Note on the History of Sociology in Reply to Professor Karl Pearson," in *Sociological Papers* by Francis Galton *et al.* (London: Macmillan, 1905), Vol. 1, 33*n*.

50 Small, "Fifty years of Sociology in the U.S.," p. 222.

51 A. W. Small, "Sociology and Plato's *Republic*," *American Journal of Sociology*, XXX (1924-25c).

52 Louis Wirth, "Fifty Years of Sociology," *American Journal of Sociology Index, 1895-1947* (1947), p. 274.

53 Small, "Fifty Years of Sociology in the U.S.," p. 254.

54 Barnes, "Albion W. Small and Modern Sociology," pp. 43-44.

55 Small, "The Methodology of the Social Problem," pp. 114, 131.

56 A. W. Small, "The Subject-Matter of Sociology," *American Journal of Sociology*, X (1904), 295.

57 Small, *The Meaning of Social Science*, pp. 200, 203, 227.

58 A. W. Small, "The Present Outlook of Social Science," *American Journal of Sociology*, XVIII (1912-13), 469.

59 Small, n.d., p. 10.

II Sketch for a Critical History of Anthropology

1 I. C. Jarvie, *The Revolution in Anthropology* (New York: Humanities Press, 1964).

2 A. I. Hallowell, "The History of Anthropology as an Anthropological Problem," *Journal of the History of the Behavioral Sciences*, I (1965), 24-38.

3 Georges Gusdorf, *Introduction aux sciences humaines: essai critique sur leurs et leur développement* (Paris: Les Belles Lettres, 1960), p. 150.

4 *Ibid.*, p. 146.

5 Paul Topinard, *Éléments d'anthropologie générale.* (Paris: 1885).

6 Gusdorf, p. 160, n. 3.

7 *Ibid.*, pp. 321-322.

8 Immanuel Kant, *Anthropologie*, 1798, trans. J. Tissot (Paris: 1863).

9 Gusdorf, pp. 393-394.

10 Topinard, p. 176.

11 U. G. Weatherly, "Racial Pessimism," *Publications of the American Sociological Society*, XVIII (1923), 1-17.

12 Robert Redfield, *Human Nature and the Study of Society: The Papers*

of Robert Redfield, Vol. 1, ed. Margaret Park Redfield (Chicago: University of Chicago, 1962) p. 5.

13   Franz Boas, "History of Anthropology," *St. Louis Congress of Arts and Science,* V (1904), 477.

14   M. Herskovits, *Franz Boas* (New York: Charles Scribner's Sons, 1953), p. 68.

15   *Ibid.,* p. 69.

16   K. O. L. Burridge, "Culture and Personality and History: A Review," *Journal of World History,* IX (1965), 21, 29.

17   Herskovits, p. 70.

18   Edward E. Evans-Pritchard, "Social Anthropology: Past and Present," *Man,* L (1950), No. 198, 122-124.

19   Edward E. Evans-Pritchard, *Anthropology and History* (Manchester: University Press, 1961).

20   Redfield, *Human Nature and the Study of Society,* p. 11.

21   *Ibid.,* p. 112.

22   *Ibid.,* p. 118.

23   *Ibid.,* p. 118.

24   *Ibid.,* p. 121.

25   Gusdorf, *Introduction aux sciences humaines,* p. 384.

26   *Ibid.,* p. 399.

27   *Ibid.,* p. 399.

28   Boas, "History of Anthropology," p. 481.

29   *Ibid.,* p. 480.

30   *Ibid.,* p. 472.

31   *Ibid.,* pp. 480-481.

32   *Ibid.,* p. 481.

33   *Ibid.,* p. 478.

34   Herskovits, *Franz Boas,* pp. 121-122.

35   Boas, "History of Anthropology," p. 482.

36   George Stocking, "Franz Boas and the Culture Concept in Historical Perspective" *American Anthropologist,* LXVIII (1966), 867-882.

37   R. H. Lowie, *Lowie's Selected Papers in Anthropology,* ed. Cora du Bois (Berkeley: University of California Press, 1960), p. 489.

38   *Ibid.,* p. 490.

39   *Ibid.,* p. 493.

40   *Ibid.,* p. 410.

41   *Ibid.,* p. 483.

42   *Ibid.,* pp. 483-485 *passim.*

43   Arthur J. Vidich, introduction to Paul Radin's *The Method and Theory of Ethnology* (New York: Basic Books, 1966), pp. vii-cxv.

44   Jarvie, *The Revolution in Anthropology,* pp. 12-13.

45 Derek Freeman, review of E. R. Leach's *Rethinking Anthropology, Man* (1962), p. 126.

46 E. Adamson Hoebel, review of Evans-Pritchard's *Anthropology and History, Man* (1962), p. 125.

47 Harry Elmer Barnes, "The Development of Historical Sociology," *Publications of the American Sociological Society*, XVI (1921), 17-49.

48 Alexander Goldenweiser, "Four Phases of Anthropological Thought: An Outline," *Publications of the American Sociological Society*, XVI (1921), 65-67 passim.

49 Theodore Waitz, *Introduction to Anthropology*, trans. J. F. Collingwood (London: Longman, Green, 1863) p. xiv.

50 *Ibid.*, p. 9.

51 *Ibid.*, p. 13.

52 Samuel Butler, London, *The Press*, July 29, 1865.

53 Margaret T. Hodgen, *The Doctrine of Survivals, a Chapter in the History of Scientific Method in the Study of Man* (London: Allenson & Co., 1936), pp. 56 ff.

54 Lowie, *Selected Papers in Anthropology*, p. 406.

55 Lord Monboddo (James Burnet), *Antient Metaphysics*, Vol. 3 (London, 1784), p. 27.

56 *Ibid.*, Vol. 3, p. 222.

57 A. L. Kroeber, "Integration of the Knowledge of Man," *The Unity of Knowledge*, ed. Lewis Leary (New York: Doubleday, 1955), pp. 125-149.

58 Adam Ferguson, *History of Civil Society* (5th ed.; Edinburgh: Bell, 1782).

59 John Millar, *The Origin of the Distinction of Ranks* (Basil; Tourneisen, 1793), p. 140.

60 *Ibid.*, p. 147.

61 *Ibid.*, p. 159.

62 *Ibid.*, p. 261.

63 J. M. Robertson, *Buckle and His Critics* (London, 1895).

64 Charles Letourneaux, *Sociology Based on Ethnology* (London, 1893).

65 R. Petrucci, *Les Origines naturelles de la propriété* (Brussels, 1905).

66 Émile de Laveleye, *Primitive Property*, trans. G. Marriott (London, 1878).

67 Henry George, *Progress and Poverty* (New York: The Robert Schalkenbach Foundation, 1962).

68 Robert de Fremery, *Money and Freedom* (San Francisco: The Henry George School, 1955).

69 T. Veblen, "The Beginnings of Ownership," *American Journal of Sociology*, IV (1898–1899), 352-365.

70 Frederic Engels, *The Origin of the Family, Private Property, and the*

State in the Light of the Researches of Lewis H. Morgan (1942 ed.; New York: International Publishers), p. 6.

71 Franz Oppenheimer, *The State: Its Origin and Development Viewed Sociologically*, trans. J. M. Gitterman (Indianapolis: Bobbs-Merrill, 1912).

72 Fustel de Coulanges, *The Origin of Property in Land*, trans. Margaret Ashley (London: Swan Sonnenschein, 1891), p. 2.

73 *Ibid.,* p. 150.

74 *Ibid.,* p. 153.

75 Rudolf Holsti, *The Relation of War to the Origin of the State* (Helsingfors, 1913).

76 W. C. MacLeod, *The Origin of the State: Reconsidered in the Light of the Data on Aboriginal North America* (Ph.D. Dissertation, Philadelphia, 1924).

77 R. H. Lowie, "The Origin of the State," *The Freeman* (1922), 440-442, 465-467.

78 *Ibid.,* p. 441.

79 Robert MacIver, *The Web of Government* (New York: The Macmillan Company, 1947).

80 Lawrence Krader, *Formation of the State* (Englewood Cliffs: Prentice-Hall, 1968).

81 T. E. Cliffe Leslie, introduction to English edition of de Laveleye's *Primitive Property*, 1878, pp. xx-xxi.

82 W. C. MacLeod, *The Origin and History of Politics* (New York, 1931), p. 98.

83 *Ibid.,* p. 99.

84 *Ibid.,* p. 98.

85 Harry Elmer Barnes, "The Struggle of Races and Social Groups as a Factor in the Development of Political and Social Institutions; an Exposition and Critique of the Sociological System of Ludwig Gumplowicz," *Journal of Race Development*, V (1918), 394-419. "The Natural State of Man: An Historical Résumé of Theory," *The Monist* (1923). "Theories of the Origin of the State in Classical Political Economy," *The Monist* (1924).

86 P. N. Ure, *The Origin of Tyranny* (Cambridge, 1922).

87 Gunnar Landtman, *The Origin of Priesthood* (Ekenaes, 1905). *The Primary Causes of Social Inequality* (Helsingfors, 1908). *The Origin of the Inequality of the Social Classes* (London: Kegan Paul, 1938).

88 Benjamin Nelson, *The Idea of Usury: From Tribal Brotherhood to Universal Otherhood* (Princeton: Princeton University Press, 1949).

89 William F. Albright, *From the Stone Age to Christianity: Monotheism and the Historical Process* (2nd ed.; New York: Anchor Books), p. 101.

90 Iu. I. Semenov, "The Doctrine of Morgan, Marxism, and Contemporary Ethnography," *Soviet Anthropology and Archaeology*, IV (1965), No. 2, Fall, 3-15.

91 A. J. Penty, *A Guildsman's Interpretation of History* (London: Allen & Unwin, 1920).

92 I. Kon, "Review of *The New Sociology*," *Soviet Sociology*, IV (1965) No. 1, Summer, 53.

93 Max Weber, *The Methodology of the Social Sciences* (New York: Free Press, 1949), pp. 90 ff.

94 J. L. Myres, "Anthropology and Political Science," *Report of the British Association for the Advancement of Science* (Winnipeg, 1909), p. 615.

95 Ashley Montagu, ed., *The Concept of the Primitive* (New York: Free Press, 1968).

96 Pitirim Sorokin, *Sociological Theories of Today* (New York: Harper & Row, 1966), pp. 607-608.

97 Talcott Williams, "Was Primitive Man a Modern Savage?" *Smithsonian Institute Annual Report* (1896), pp. 541-548.

98 Edmund Stevens, "Crime in Russia's New Society—Figures Given," *San Francisco Chronicle,* November 26, 1965, p. 16.

99 A. Ia. Gurevich, "Certain Aspects of the Study of Social History (Historical Social Psychology), *The Soviet Review*, VI, No. 2 (Summer 1965), 28-44.

100 Eric Voegelin, "The Growth of the Race Idea," *The Review of Politics,* II (1940), 283-317. *The New Science of Politics* (Chicago: University of Chicago Press, 1952).

101 Albert Salomon, "Crisis, History and the Image of Man," *Review of Politics,* II (1940), 415 ff.

INDEX

174   THE LOST SCIENCE OF MAN

Journal of Folk-Psychology and Philology, 78
Journal of Social Science, 6, 21, 22, 24, 25, 28, 50
Judaeo-Christian philosophy of history, xi
Jung, Carl, 106n

Kames, Lord (Henry Home), 77, 129
Kant, Immanuel, 63, 76, 78, 79, 96, 117, 122, 123, 125, 127, 134, 141, 153, 163; *Anthropology,* 78, 163; "Conjectural Beginnings of Human History," 125
Klemm, F., 105
Kluckholn, Clyde, 102. *See also* Kroeber, Alfred L.
Knies, K., 13
Kon, I., 167
Kovalevski, Maksim, 126
Krader, Lawrence, 133, 166
Kroeber, Alfred L., 83, 102, 124n, 165; *Culture,* 102
Kuhn, T. S., 134; *The Structure of Scientific Revolutions,* 134

Lahontan, Baron de, 62, 115, 149
laissez-faire, 5, 7, 8, 9, 9n, 12, 13, 15, 16, 26, 39, 44, 126, 134
Lamarck, Jean Baptiste, 75, 76
Lamprecht, S. P., 109, 132
Landtman, Gunnar, 138, 166
La Philosophie positive, 82
Lavrov, Peter, 141
Lazarus, Moritz, 78
Leach, E. R., 165
Lee, Alfred McClung, x
Lessing, Gotthold Ephraim, 141

Letourneaux, Charles, 125, 165
Lévi-Strauss, Claude, 95, 103, 123
Linnaeus, Carolus, 75
Lotze, Rudolph Hermann, 50, 141, 145
Lowie, Robert H., 83, 84, 90, 95, 101–105, 117, 118, 120, 125, 132, 133, 138, 164, 165, 166; *Are We Civilized?,* 84
Lubbock, Sir John, 81, 125
Lynd, Robert S., 28

Mach, Ernst, 117
MacIver, Robert, 133, 136, 166
MacLeod, W. C., 133, 135, 166; *The Origin and History of Politics,* 135, 166
Maine De Biran, 125, 128
Maitland, Frederic William, 89
Malays, the, 114
Malinowski, Bronislaw, 85, 86, 95, 107
Marx, Karl, 17, 26, 31, 50, 64, 100, 117, 122, 127, 128, 129, 130, 133, 136, 140–44, 151, 152
McLennan, John Ferguson, 125
Mead, George Herbert, 63
Menger, Karl, 13
Merton, Robert, 103
Metternich, Klemens von, 137
Middle Ages, 144
Mill, John Stuart, vii, 14
Millar, John, 77, 124–25, 126, 129, 131, 134, 165; *The Origin of the Distinction of Ranks,* 124, 165
Mills, C. Wright, ix, 28, 64, 65, 66, 67, 69, 70, 134, 143, 148; *The Power Elite,* 66; *The New Sociology,* 143

153; *Emile,* 71, 73; *Discourse on the Origins of Inequality,* 122, 123
Royce, Josiah, 63, 141
Russell, Bertrand, 117
Russia, 67, 152

Saint-Hilaire, Etienne G., 76
St. Louis (Missouri), 95
Saint-Pierre, Abbé de, 51
Saint-Simon, Claude, 31, 37, 50, 52, 79, 96
Salomon, Albert, 154, 167
Santayana, George, 91, 155
São Paulo (Brazil), 67
Sapir, Edward, 83
Savigny, Friedrich Karl von, 13
Schaeffle, Albert, 14, 17, 18
Schelling, Friedrich W. J. von, 112
Schmidt, W., 103
Schmoller, Gustav, 14
Schumpeter, Joseph Alois, 53, 162
Science and Society, 9n
Seebohm, Frederick, 126
Seebohm, Hugh, 126
Seligman, Edwin R. A., 136
Semaine de Synthèse, 139n
Semenov, Iu. I., 140, 167
Shotwell, James T., 109
Simmel, Georg, 63
Small, Albion Woodbury, ix–x, 1–70 *passim,* 95, 97, 98, 99, 100, 101, 161, 162, 163; *Adam Smith and Modern Sociology: A Study in the Methodology of the Social Sciences,* 10, 63, 161; *The Cameralists: The Pioneers of German Social Polity,* 12, 63; "Conflict of Classes," 64; "The

Present Outlook of Social Science," 13, 163; *The Origins of Sociology,* 13, 63; *Between Eras from Capitalism to Democracy,* 13, 63; *The Meaning of Social Science,* 21, 41, 49, 162
Smith, Adam, 11, 12, 13–14, 79, 125, 126, 127, 134, 142
Smith, Dusky Lee, 9n
"Socialism of the Chair," 47
Society of Anthropology, 78
Society of the Observers of Man, 78
Socrates, 156, 157
Sorokin, Pitirim, 28, 34, 59, 150, 167
Soviets, the, 140–43
Sozialpolitik, 15, 32, 43, 49
Spencer, Herbert, 15, 17, 18, 63, 66, 81, 96, 97, 114, 125, 126
Steinhausen, Georg, 109
Steinthal, Heymann, 78. *See* Lazarus, Moritz
Stevens, Edmund, 167
Steward, Julian H., 103, 140
Stocking, George, 100, 164

Tawney, R. H., 9
Teggart, Frederick J., 4
Teilhard de Chardin, P., 94
Thomas, W. I., 138
Thuringians the, 132
Thurnwald, Richard, 102
Tillich, Paul, 147, 154
Topinard, Paul, 77, 79, 163
Turner, Frederick Jackson, 109
Tylor, Sir Edward B., 81, 83, 86, 96, 97, 103, 105, 114, 125, 126